Landscapes of
LA PALMA
AND EL HIERRO

a countryside guide
Eighth edition

Noel Rochford
updated by Conny Spelbrink

SUNFLOWER BOOKS

Eighth edition © 2020
Sunflower Books™
PO Box 36160
London SW7 3WS, UK
www.sunflowerbooks.co.uk

All rights reserved. No part of this publication may be reproduced, stored in a retrieval system, or transmitted by any form or by any means, electronic, mechanical, photocopying, recording or otherwise, without the prior written permission of the publishers.

Sunflower Books and 'Landscapes' are Registered Trademarks.

ISBN 978-1-85691-530-4

Salinas at Fuencaliente (Walk 16)

Important note to the reader

We have tried to ensure that the descriptions and maps in this book are error-free at press date. The book will be updated, where necessary, in future editions. It will be very helpful for us to receive your comments (sent to info@sunflowerbooks.co.uk, please) for the updating of future editions.

We also rely on those who use this book — especially walkers — to take along a good supply of common sense when they explore. Conditions can change fairly rapidly in the western Canaries, and ***storm damage or bulldozing may make a route unsafe at any time***. If the route is not as we outline it here, and your way ahead is not secure, return to the point of departure. ***Never attempt to complete a tour or walk under hazardous conditions!*** Please read carefully the notes on pages 32-39, and the introductory comments at the beginning of each tour and walk (regarding road conditions, equipment, grade, distances, time). Explore ***safely***, and at the same time respect the beauty of the countryside.

Cover photograph: Caldera de Taburiente (Walk 20)
Title page: sabina (Juniperus phoenicea, *a native juniper*)

Shutterstock: 1, 2, 14-5, 22, 24-5, 33, 46, 49, 58-9, 62, 64-5, 100, 111, 115, 116, 122-3, 126, 128-9, 132-3, 136, 141, 147, 150; Conny Spelbrink: 16-7, 36, 40-1, 67, 69, 70, 77, 81, 91, 93, 103, 110, 112-3, 135, 144; all others: Noel Rochford
Maps: Nick Hill for Sunflower Books. Base map data © OpenStreetMap contributors. Contour data made available under ODbL (opendatacommons.org/licenses/odbl/1.0)
Drawings: Sharon Rochford
A CIP catalogue record for this book is available from the British Library.
Printed and bound in England: Short Run Press, Exeter

Contents

Preface	5
Acknowledgements; Recommended reading; Useful websites	6
Getting about	7
Picnicking	8
Picnic suggestions on La Palma	9
Picnic suggestions on El Hierro	10
Touring	11
LA PALMA'S VERDANT NORTH AND THE ISLAND'S SUMMITS (Tour 1)	13
Santa Cruz • Los Sauces • Barlovento • Garafía • Roque de los Muchachos • Santa Cruz	
VOLCANIC SPLENDOURS IN THE SOUTH OF LA PALMA (Tour 2)	19
Santa Cruz • Los Canarios (Fuencaliente) • El Paso • El Pilar • Santuario de las Nieves • Santa Cruz	
CALDERA DE TABURIENTE (Tour 3)	24
Los Llanos • Caldera de Taburiente • Barranco de las Angustias • Los Brecitos • Tazacorte • Mirador El Time • (Puntagorda) • Los Llanos	
EL HIERRO — HIGHLIGHTS (Tour 4)	26
Tigaday • Sabinosa • La Dehesa • (Faro de Orchilla) • Cruz de los Reyes • Hoya del Morcillo • El Pinar • Cala de Tacorón • Mirador de las Playas • Mirador de Jinama • Mirador de la Peña • Mocanal • Pozo de las Calcosas • Valverde • San Andrés • Tigaday	
Walking (● see explanation of grading symbols on page 33)	32
Grading, waymarking, maps, GPS	32
Where to stay	34
What to take	35
Weather	35
Dogs — and other nuisances	35
Country code	37
Advice for walkers	37
Spanish for walkers	38
Organisation of the walks	39
WALKS ON LA PALMA	40
● 1 From the Mirador La Tosca to Gallegos	42
● 2 Los Sauces • Mirador de las Barandas • Barlovento	45
● 3 Las Lomadas • Barranco del Agua • Los Tilos • Los Sauces	48
● 4 Two viewpoints from Los Tilos	52
● 5 Casa del Monte • Nacientes de Cordero • Nacientes de Marcos • Los Tilos	54

4　Landscapes of La Palma and El Hierro

- 6 Casa del Monte • Nacientes de Cordero • Casa del Monte • Las Lomadas — 59
- 7 Barranco de la Galga — 63
- 8 Cubo de la Galga circuit — 65
- 9 Puntallana springs — 67
- 10 Puntallana, short and sassy — 69
- 11 From Tenagua through the jungle to the *lavaderos* in the Barranco del Agua — 71
- 12 LP4 (Pico de la Nieve turn-off) • Pico de la Nieve • La Cumbrecita • Ermita de la Virgen del Pino • National Park Visitors' Centre — 74
- 13 From La Cumbrecita to the Ermita de la Virgen del Pino and the National Park Visitors' Centre — 80
- 14 Lomo de los Mestres • La Pared Vieja • Refugio El Pilar • National Park Visitors' Centre — 83
- 15 Lomo de los Mestres • La Pared Vieja • Cumbre Nueva • Camino de la Faya • Mazo — 87
- 16 Los Canarios (Fuencaliente) • Volcán de San Antonio • Volcán de Teneguía • Faro de Fuencaliente — 90
- 17 Ruta de los Volcanes — 95
- 18 Birigoyo, or Ruta de los Volcanes 'lite' — 101
- 19 Pico Bejenado — 102
- 20 Caldera de Taburiente from Los Brecitos — 104
- 21 Barranco de las Angustias and the Cascada de Colores — 110
- 22 From the Mirador El Time to Puerto de Tazacorte — 112
- 23 Tijarafe • Poris de Candelaria (the 'Pirates' Cove') • Tijarafe — 114
- 24 From Tijarafe to Tinizara — 117
- 25 El Fayal • Las Tricias • Cuevas de Buracas • Las Tricias — 121
- 26 Garafía • El Palmar • Juan Adalid • El Palmar • Garafía — 125

WALKS ON EL HIERRO — 132

- 27 From the Pista al Derrabado to Sabinosa — 130
- 28 Sabinosa • Mirador de Bascos • El Sabinar • Ermita de los Reyes • Sabinosa — 132
- 29 Coastal walk at Arenas Blancas — 135
- 30 Frontera • Mirador de Jinama • Ermita Virgen de la Peña • Mirador de la Peña — 137
- 31 Frontera • Mirador de Jinama • San Andrés — 140
- 32 Circuit from the Fuente de la Llanía — 143
- 33 From San Andrés to the Arbol Garoé — 145
- 34 Fuente de la Llanía • Mirador de las Playas • La Torre • San Andrés — 148
- 35 Fuente de la Llanía • Mirador de Isora • Parador — 152

Some plants you may see on these islands   150, 151
Bus timetables, flights and ferries   155
Index   159
Fold-out touring maps   *inside back cover*
(with plans of Santa Cruz de La Palma and Valverde)

🌻 Preface

For most tourists in Britain, the Canary Islands mean Tenerife, Gran Canaria, Lanzarote and Fuerteventura. But there are actually seven islands in the archipelago. Lesser-known La Gomera, La Palma and El Hierro are still utopias for nature lovers. They are still quite unspoilt.

They lack the fine glistening beaches of the more popular islands, and this may be their saving grace. It's unlikely that mainstream tourism will ever reach them. Great news for those of us who seek peace and quiet.

In natural beauty, La Palma rivals all the other islands put together. Its immense, abyss-like crater, the Caldera de Taburiente (which geologists now refer to as an enormous landslide), is one of the largest of its kind in the world. Deep within its pine-speckled, towering walls is a year-round abundance of water — gushing streams, boisterous cascades, and a plummeting waterfall. Outside the crater, high on the cloud-catching hillsides, two million-year-old laurel forests grow as dense as jungle. In the southern half of the island, hills pitted with volcanic craters, and mini-deserts of black *lapilli* speak of the island's volcanic past. This stark, striking landscape, all the more dramatic for its stabs of volcanic reds, oranges, and yellows, is far removed from the lush and verdant, tree-clad north.

In the southern half of La Palma the stark volcanic landscape is enlivened by stabs of volcanic reds — and nowhere more so than around Volcán Martín with its reddish-pink cone and luminous green pines dotting the foreground (Walk 17).

6 Landscapes of La Palma and El Hierro

Landing on El Hierro by boat many years ago, I wondered what I had let myself in for. Before me rose a dried-up, sprawling mountain of rock, climbing straight out of the sea, treeless and barren. Tired stone walls stretched half-heartedly across steep sea slopes ... the only hint of civilization. But day by day the island's charms revealed themselves: dramatic cliff top views, highland pastures shrouded in mist, countryside littered with volcanic cones, a maze of stone walls, turquoise-green rock pools, delightful rustic villages, venerable Canary pines and wizened junipers. These were but a few of the island's unpublicized treasures. And where else would your taxi driver buy *you* lunch? Still little touched by tourism, El Hierro is by far the friendliest place in the Canaries.

If you want a holiday with razzmatazz, head for one of the 'big four' (with the appropriate *Landscapes* guide). But if you don't mind unrushed service, and if you want to return home more relaxed than when you left, then start packing. Discover La Gomera with *Landscapes of Gomera and Southern Tenerife*, or use this book to enjoy the best of La Palma and El Hierro.

Acknowledgements
Special thanks to the following people for their invaluable help: Conny Spelbrink, who lives on La Palma, checking the walks regularly, revising them and contributing new routes; the Oficina de Turismo, El Hierro; Medio Ambiente, La Palma and El Hierro; my sister Sharon, for her illustrations of island flora.

Recommended reading
There are several guides in English for both islands: you'll find the widest selection in souvenir- and bookshops on the islands themselves. For a wonderful guide to wild flowers and the local vegetation, try to buy a copy of Bramwell's *Wild flowers of the Canary Islands* on the islands, or look for it in your library or online.

Useful websites
www.visitlapalma.es (La Palma Tourist Board)
www.senderosdelapalma.es (official website of the island's marked trails, with updates on any closures)
www.hellocanaryislands.com (official website of the Canary Islands)
www.elhierro.es (El Hierro Tourist Board)
www.iac.es (observatory website; see photo caption on page 16)
www.reservasparquesnacionales.es (to book parking and camping in the national park, and to see trail updates)
www.parador.es (government-run hotels; see page 34)
www.islabonita.com (country cottages; see page 34)
See also pages 7 and 155 for bus, flight and ferry websites.

Getting about

There is no doubt that a **hired car** is the most convenient way of getting about on these islands, and I definitely recommend it on El Hierro (where there are very few bus lines); it's the most convenient way to get around La Palma as well. If you *do* hire a car, GPS coordinates for parking places are shown under 'Transport' for each walk, so that you can set your sat nav (or smartphone). When hiring, ask to see all the rental and insurance conditions (in English), and carry the rental firm's telephone number (and out-of-office-hours number) with you. If you pay by credit card, remember to check the amount you sign for and keep all receipts!

The second most flexible form of transport is a hired **taxi** and, especially if three or four people are sharing the cost, this becomes an attractive idea. If you're making an unmetered journey, do agree on the price *before* setting out: all taxi drivers should carry an official price list.

Coach tours are the most popular way of seeing many holiday islands; this is an easy way to get to know a place in comfort, before embarking on your own adventures.

My favourite way of getting about is by **local bus**. The system is very economical and reliable, and the bus network on La Palma is good — although the same can not be said for El Hierro. Plans of Santa Cruz and Valverde with the maps at the back of the book show you where to board buses in these towns. Timetables for all the buses used for the walks and picnics are on pages 155-158. But please do not rely *solely* on these timetables: pick up the latest bus timetables from the bus stations or, better, download them before you travel.

La Palma's bus company is called TILP (Transportes Insular La Palma). Their website, **tilp.es**, has no English version at present, but it is very easy to see the timetables: click on 'Líneas Regulares', then 'Líneas y horarios'. You can download timetables with route maps by clicking on 'Descargar las líneas y horarios'. There are *no* special fare-saving tickets for visitors as we go to press, but prices are reasonable and depend on distance travelled: up to 10km for €1.50, 10-20km for €2.40, over 20km for €2.60.

El Hierro may have fewer buses but TransHierro, the operator, *does* have an English website: **transhierro.net**, where you can check all their timetables and routes. The price per journey is €1.60; saver tickets cost €13 for 15 trips.

Picnicking

La Palma and El Hierro are rugged and unspoilt, ideal for picnicking. On the following pages I have listed a few of my favourite picnic spots along the routes of the walks. All the information you need to get there is given on the following pages, where *picnic numbers correspond to walk numbers*. So you can quickly find the general location on the islands by referring to the touring maps, where the walks are numbered in green. I give transport details (🚗: car parking; 🚌: how to get there by bus), walking times, and views or setting. Beside the picnic title, you will find a map reference: the location of the picnic spot is pinpointed on this *walking map* with the symbol **P**. Many of the picnic places are illustrated.

Most of these picnic spots are reached after a very short, easy walk. In fact, they make *excellent rambles for 'non-walkers'*, and are ideal for stretching your legs during car tours. Do, however, look over the comments before setting out: if some walking is involved, remember to wear sensible shoes. Always take a **sunhat** with you (○ indicates a picnic in full sun). It's a good idea to take along a plastic sheet as well, in case the ground is damp or prickly.

La Palma

1 MIRADOR LA TOSCA (map page 42, photo page 44)

by car: 15-25min on foot
by bus: 20-30min on foot

🚗 Park in the space next to the Mirador La Tosca (28° 48.642'N, 17° 48.871'W; Car tour 1).
🚌 bus to the Mirador La Tosca (Línea 120 from Barlovento)

Follow the beginning of Walk 1, down to a magnificent panorama over La Tosca and the distant sea-cliffs. Dragon trees galore; shade nearby.

3 LOS TILOS (map page 48, photos pages 50, 51) 🍴

by car: 5-30min on foot
by bus: not easily accessible

🚗 Park at Los Tilos car park (28° 47.388'N, 17° 48.130'W; Car tour 1).

Below the visitors' centre there is an organised picnic area — quiet except for weekends. But I prefer picnicking below it, alongside the watercourse (canal). To get there, refer to the notes in Walk 3, from the 2h-point at the Interpretation Centre. It's an excellent spot. Then perhaps refer to Short walk 3 to explore the fascinating barranco (which I find too busy with walking traffic for an enjoyable picnic).

12 ERMITA DE LA VIRGEN DEL PINO (photo page 22, map page 75)

by car: 5-20min on foot
by bus: not easily accessible

🚗 Park in the car park at the chapel: take the LP302 for 'Parque Nacional'; the first right turn leads to the *ermita*. (28° 39.773'N, 17° 50.506W; Car tour 2)

Picnic in the forest of venerable Canary pines behind the chapel.

14a LA PARED VIEJA (map page 85) 🍴

by car: up to 5min on foot
by bus: not easily accessible

🚗 Park at the picnic area. Turn left off the El Pilar/San Isidro road just under 5km northeast of the Refugio El Pilar (signposted). (28° 37.110'N, 17° 49.386W; Car tour 2)

An official picnic site in a dense laurel forest. Popular on weekends.

14b (REFUGIO) EL PILAR (map page 85, photo page 96) 🍴

by car: up to 5min on foot   by bus: not easily accessible

🚗 Park at the picnic area, off the El Pilar road (LP301), 7km south of the LP3 (28° 36.845'N, 17° 50.191'W; Car tour 2).

An official picnic site in the woods at

Not all picnic places need be on the route of walks: what more pleasant than to sit by this spring and shrine to St John the Baptist at Puntallana?

Picnic suggestions   9

the foot of Pico Birigoyo. Children's playground, visitors' centre, etc. Very busy on weekends and in the summer

14c LLANO DEL JABLE (map page 85, photo pages 84-85)

by car: up to 5min on foot
by bus: not easily accessible
🚗 Park under the pines: turn right off the El Pilar road onto a gravel track just beyond Montaña Quemada, 4km south of the LP3 (28° 37.360'N, 17° 50.559'E; a detour on Car tour 2).
Picnic under pines in this 'desert' of black lapilli. Avoid on windy days.

21 CALDERA DE TABURIENTE (map page 111, photo page 105) ○

by car: 20-40min on foot
🚗 Park in the bed of the Barranco de las Angustias (28° 41.144'N, 17° 54.570'W; Car tour 3).
Picnic anywhere along the barranco. Some 20 minutes upstream, you will find water in the river bed. There is some shade from the ravine walls about 40 minutes upstream, by a small cascade and pool.

Some recommended organised picnic sites on La Palma

LAGUNA DE BARLOVENTO (map page 46, photo page 47; Car tour 1) △✕🚗

🚗 Park at the picnic site. Follow the LP109 southwest from Barlovento for 2km, then fork left to the picnic area.
Official site with full facilities, plus restaurant, camp ground.

EL FAYAL (map page 123; Car tour 3) 🚗

🚗 Park at the site: turn left off the LP1 (signposted for Puntagorda) 1.5km north of the main Puntagorda turn-off (the turn-off to the picnic site is also the rear entrance to the village.
Located amidst pines and tree heather; full facilities.

MONTE BREÑA (touring map; Car tour 2) 🚗

🚗 Park at the site, off the LP202 south of San José.
An official site with full facilities.

El Hierro

30a MIRADOR DE JINAMA (map page 138, photo page 141)

by car: 5-15min on foot
by bus: not easily accessible
🚗 Park at the *mirador* (27° 45.801'N, 17° 58.838'E; Car tour 4).
Picnic on the hillside above the mirador, in the shade of pines. Or follow the path down towards Frontera for ten minutes, where you will find a belvedere with stone tables and benches (but no shade). There are stunning views here, but the return is steep.

30b ERMITA VIRGEN DE LA PEÑA (map page 138, photo page 139) ○

by car: 20-30min on foot
by bus: 20-30min on foot
🚗 Park at the Mirador de la Peña (27° 48.478'N, 17° 58.774'W; Car tour 4) and walk up to the *ermita*.
🚌 Guarazoca bus (Línea 5) to the end of the route
Picnic alongside the chapel, overlooking El Golfo. One of the finest views in the archipelago, but very little shade.

32 MIRADOR DE LA LLANIA (map page 144, photo page 144)

by car: 5-10min on foot
by bus: not easily accessible

Picnic suggestions

🚗 Park alongside the HI1 at the turn-off to the Ermita Virgen de los Reyes by the Fuente de la Llanía (27° 44.174'N, 17° 59.812'W; Car tour 4).
Follow the sign for the mirador and climb to the rim of the cumbre, for more stunning views over the crater. Use the notes for Walk 32 to see the exquisite wooded paths in the area. Plenty of shade nearby.

34 MIRADOR DE LAS PLAYAS (map page 149, photo page 150)

by car: up to 5min on foot
by bus: 20-30min on foot
🚗 Park at the the *mirador*: the turn-off lies south of San Andrés, 5km down the El Pinar/La Restinga road (27° 43.909'N, 17° 58.303'W; Car tour 4).
🚌 Línea 2: alight at the turn-off to the *mirador*, 700m away.
Picnic near the mirador, with its superb coastal view. Shade of pines.

Some recommended organised picnic sites on El Hierro

LAS PLAYAS (see touring map) 🏕

🚗 Park off the HI30 at Las Playas, 1.5km north of the *parador*.
An organised site with a spectacular backdrop.

TIMIJIRAQUE (see touring map) 🏕

🚗 Park at the site, off the HI30 south of Puerto de la Estaca
Located at one of the few sandy beaches on the island.

HOYA DEL MORCILLO (see touring map) 🏕

🚗 Park at the picnic area, described in Car tour 4, page 33.

CALA DE TACORÓN (photo page 30; see touring map) 🏕

🚗 Park at Cala de Tacorón, described in Car tour 4, page 33.

HOYA DEL PINO (see touring map) 🏕

🚗 Park at the site, off the HI1, southwest of Frontera
Surrounded by laurel forest

CHARCO MANSO (see touring map) 🏕

🚗 Park at Charco Manso, a detour on Car tour 4
Delightful sea pools, fireplaces and other facilities

LA MACETA (map pages 116 117) 🏕

🚗 Park at La Maceta, north of Frontera
Good facilities; barbecues and pools

PLAYA DEL VERODAL (see touring map) 🏕

🚗 Park at Playa del Verodal, described in Car tour 4, page 30.

PUERTO DE ORCHILLA (see touring map) 🏕

🚗 Park at Puerto de Orchilla, a detour on Car tour 4; see page 30.

Touring

Car hire on these islands is good value, especially if you book online before travelling. **Roads** vary from quite wide 'A'-type (there are *no* motorways!) to winding and precipitous — and then there are the gravel tracks of El Hierro's highlands. Road conditions are described at the top of each tour.

There are three tours on La Palma: I've simply split the island north and south, but devoted a full day to the Caldera de Taburiente and surrounding landscapes. El Hierro's highlights *can* all be seen in a day ... but naturally, I hope you'll take a wrong turning somewhere — not only on Hierro, but on both islands. The serendipity of 'getting lost' is, after all, the best way to get to know a place.

The touring notes are brief: they include little history or other information that you can obtain in general guides or free from the local tourist offices. Instead, I've concentrated on the 'logistics' of touring: times and distances, road conditions, and seeing parts of the islands that many tourists miss. Most of all, I emphasise possibilities for **walking** and **picnicking** (the symbol *P* is used to alert you to a picnic spot; see pages 8-11). While some of the picnic and short walk suggestions may not be suitable during a long car tour, you may see a landscape that you would like to explore at leisure another day.

Most major **petrol stations** are open on Sundays and holidays, but a few of the smaller ones may not be. Take along **warm clothing** and some **food and drink**; be prepared for delays on the small country roads and tracks, and remember that mountain roads may sometimes be **impassable** in stormy weather.

Allow ample time for stops: my times include only short breaks at viewpoints labelled 📷 in the notes. Calculate time for **detours** as well: villages, picnics and walks shown in ( ) at the top of the tours are only accessible via *detours*. Distances quoted are *cumulative km from the departure towns.*

The touring maps are designed to be held out facing the touring notes and contain all the information you need to follow the tours. But take time to look at the walking maps, too, when touring; they cover much of the islands in greater detail. The **symbols** in the text correspond to those on the touring maps: see the map keys.

Car tour 1: LA PALMA'S VERDANT NORTH AND THE ISLAND'S SUMMITS

Santa Cruz • Los Sauces • Barlovento • Garafía • Roque de los Muchachos • Santa Cruz

189km/117mi; 7h driving; take the northern exit from Santa Cruz. On route: ᗓ at Los Tilos, Laguna de Barlovento; Picnics (see pages 8-11) 1, 3; Walks 1-12, 25, 26

The roads are generally very winding and, on a few stretches, narrow; some are country lanes, others might prove vertiginous for some motorists. This drive is not recommended immediately after heavy rainfall (especially in winter), due to the danger of rockfall. Where the road climbs above 600m, there's always the possibility of cloud. There is only one petrol station between Barlovento and Santa Cruz — at the turn off for San Antonio del Monte, just after La Zarza (92km on the touring route via the observatory). Be alert for ongoing roadworks in the north, also for livestock and pedestrians on all roads: drive slowly.

Opening hours
El Tendal Archaeological Park daily 10.00-18.00 (15.00 Sun/Mon)
Los Tilos Interpretation Centre free admission; daily from 09.00-17.00; tel 922 451246
Parque Cultural La Zarza admission €2, children half price; daily from 11.00-17.00, closed Mondays; tel 922 695005
Observatorio Astrofísico open to the public for visits of between 70 and 90 minutes which must be booked in advance; see the observatory's website: www.iac.es.

Gaping, deep *barrancos* leave you in awe as you edge along the island's high sea shelf. The further north you go, the more desolate the landscape. Then, heading inland, you climb to the rim of the crater, up through forest, to a moonscape of volcanic hues and unsurpassed panoramic views. It will be a long day, so take plenty of snacks ... and don't forget your camera.

Heading north on the LP1 out of Santa Cruz, climb to the island's midriff (⛽ at 7.5km). At **Punta-llana** (10km ✝⊕; Walks 9-11) fork right into the village and just before the church of St John the Baptist (shown on page 70) descend a steep narrow lane to the right.* Park 0.2km downhill, off the road, just before a T-junction. Traditional Canarian houses line the lane. Ivy and other creepers cascade down the ravine walls. Walk downhill a minute, then take the first right, to find the splendid little jacaranda-shaded *plaza* shown on pages 8-9 hidden in the *barranco* wall. A spring flows into pools here, by a shrine to St John.

Return to the LP1 and continue north, heading in and out of sheer-sided ravines and a series of tunnels. Less than 1km beyond **La Galga** (17km ✕), approaching a bend in the road, pull over right for the **El Tendal Park Visitors' Centre** (★) and the **Mirador de San Bartolomé** (🖼). You pass the eponymous church (✝) as you walk up the hill. From the *mirador* there is a fine view inland, across the mountainous eastern wall that flanks the crater. Los Sauces is the settlement further north.

---
*Or park at the church and walk down

14   Landscapes of La Palma and El Hierro

Stop off at the church of San Bartolomé for a slightly unnerving cliff-edge view into the **Barranco de la Galga** (📷), then return to the main road and turn right. The track forking left just before the second tunnel is the base for Walks 7 and 8, popular walks in the laurel woods. Beyond this second tunnel another spectacular *mirador* awaits you, on the opposite side of the Barranco de la Galga. The oldest Guanche remains on La Palma, dating back to the 4th century BC, were discovered in the cave-like rock overhang you can see in the next big ravine, the **Barranco de San Juan**. The finds from this cave are exhibited in the museum at the San Francisco Convent in Santa Cruz.

At **Las Lomadas** (26.5km ✕) you reach a junction. Straight ahead is one of the most modern arched bridges (★) in the world, the spectacular span 150m/500ft above the *barranco* bed shown on page 49. But *turn left* here, for 'Los Tilos'. Immediately, a road signposted 'Los Nacientes' turns left uphill — to Los Nacientes (springs) de Marcos y Cordero — the first 8km on tarmac, then a rough track only suitable and only permitted for four-wheel-drive vehicles. Walk 6 ends at the top of the track, emerging from the canyon that hides these mountain springs: if you're adventurous, fit and have a head for heights, make Walk 5 or 6 a priority.

But for this tour keep to the main road and drive up another gaping *barranco*, the Barranco del Agua. This immense dark ravine (see photo on page 53) boasts a magnificent jungle-thick laurel forest; there is also a colony of prehistoric *Woodwardia radicans* (ferns) on the gorge wall. You can

Car tour 1: La Palma's verdant north and the island's summits

learn more about La Palma's flora at the Visitors' Centre at **Los Tilos★** (30km *i*✕☐; Picnic 3), and read more about this area on pages 48-62 (Walks 3-6).

Leaving the Barranco del Agua, continue north on the LP1 to La Palma's third largest town, **Los Sauces** (32km ✝▲✕☐⊕), where Walk 2 begins and Walk 3 ends. This very pleasant (and principal) agricultural centre is swallowed up in banana groves. Some 1.5km out of town, branch off seaward for 'San Andrés'. Descending through banana groves, you pass the signposted turn-off for Puerto Espíndola and Charco Azul, your route on the way back.

San Andrés (36km ✝▲✕) sits on the hillside just above the sea. There are two good restaurants here in the church square. Wander along the cobbled lanes of the village, then peek inside the 17th-century church in the palm-graced *plaza*, to see some rather macabre wax models. These represent ailing or injured parts of the body. In a practice dating back to the Middle Ages, they are pinned to a board on the church wall, in the hope that illnesses will be cured and injuries mended.

Return to the Puerto Espíndola junction and turn right; 0.5km further on, fork right again for 'Charco Azul'. Some 0.3km down this narrow lane, you come to a parking bay overlooking this emerald-green natural rock-pool *(charco)*, set at the foot of low sea cliffs. *(Remember, however: when the seas are high, it's too dangerous even to venture down onto the rock here.)* Continuing on through banana groves, reach a junction and turn right into the new port of **Puerto Espíndola** (39.5km ✕), with an excellent restaurant, Meson del Mar.

Ascending to the LP1, keep right. Just over 2km north along the LP1 turn right for 'Faro de Punta Cumplida'. This narrow, winding and bumpy road will take you down to some more rock pools. Keep right at the T-junction; 1.2km down, at **Punta Talavera**, there's an inconspicuous little port concealed in a rocky promontory. Park above it and walk down to the fishermen's huts that snuggle below, and to the tunnel in the rock — a very scenic spot. Swimming is only safe here when the sea is calm.

After passing the **Faro de Punta Cumplida** (▲▲), now a luxury hotel, you climb through extensive banana plantations to a T-junction, where you turn right and descend (🚗) to the **Piscinas**

Central plaza *and church of San Salvador in Santa Cruz*

The Observatorio Astrofísico, near the Roque de los Muchachos, is the most important in the northern hemisphere. For fascinating details and information about visiting (in English), log on to www.iac.es.

de la Fajana (50km ♦✗△). The pools here, larger than those at the Charco Azul, are also set in the seashore lava and are equally dangerous when the sea is high. The restaurant next to the pools has a good selection of fish and seafood, and the terrace setting is spectacular, overlooking the wild cliffs of the north coast. Walking beyond the apartments for 10 minutes, you will find some unfrequented natural pools set in a flat tongue of rough lava.

To rejoin the LP1, pass the turn-off left back to the lighthouse and keep straight uphill, ignoring all turn-offs. Turn right on the LP1 and climb to **Barlovento** (57.5km ♣✗🛒⊕), an exposed, windswept village with a thoroughfare the width of a motorway. Walk 2 ends here. Pass the LP1 off right to Gallegos and continue straight ahead for 1km, *past* the Hotel La Palma Romantica (58.5km ⌂). When you come to La Pradera (59.5km ✗), a large prettified shed standing amidst trees off to the right, you may wish to 'go native': this popular local restaurant is a brilliant lunch or snack stop. Try the excellent grilled cheese with *mojo* sauce and a glass of red wine. Just past the restaurant, take the turn-off left to the **Laguna de Barlovento** *zona recreativa* (🎋✗), laid out at the side of the island's largest reservoir, with a restaurant and duck pond (photo on page 46). All sorts of birds gather in this area around the reservoir, and in the winter one can see many migrating birds as well.

Turn back from the picnic grounds and retrace your route for 3km, then fork left on the LP1 for 'Gallegos/Franceses'. Less than 1.5km further on is the **Mirador La Tosca** (65.5km 📷; Picnic 1), from where you have a superb view over La Tosca's dragon trees and along the wild north coast. Settlements are few and far between. Grazing is the main means of livelihood in this far-flung corner of the island. Walk 1, which starts here, gives you a taste of this pastoral corner of the north.

Possible detours: The main tour passes above two precious little villages, Gallegos and Franceses. But I highly recommend taking detours to them: 2km for Gallegos and just over 5km for Franceses. Note that some of the roads are narrow and, in Franceses, some stretches of road are *vertiginous*. To make for Gallegos, where Walk 1 ends, turn right at 71.5km. Keep right on entering the village, then turn sharp left in the village centre (the first left turn you come to), ignore a road to the right and climb back up to the LP1. (But see the footnote on page 43 and map

16

on page 42: if the new *mirador* is signposted, drive down to the coast before leaving!)

The flimsy sign announcing the Franceses turn off (75km) comes up without warning. *This detour is only recommended for confident drivers.* It's a spectacular and rugged corner of the island, and relatively unvisited ... so far! You'll pass various tiny *barrios* (parts of the village), each of them named. First you squeeze through Los Machines. Then, winding in and out of gullies, ignore a turn-off to La Fajana (although it is only 2.5km off the LP1, this very narrow road down to the coast is brilliant but pretty hair-raising!). Less than 1km further on, you round a bend at the edge of the enormous Barranco Franceses and come upon a magnificent vista across the coastal hills of the northwest. Then a steep climb takes you back up to the LP1, where you turn right.

The road snakes up through tree heather to 1100m/3600ft. Keep straight on, where the LP109 joins from the left. If you're ready for lunch, visit the simple Bar/Restaurant Los Reyes in the tiny hamlet of **Roque del Faro**, 1.5km along. On cold days try the broth, the warming rabbit or goat stews, or the very tasty *gofio* dish (made from roasted maize). Wash it down with the wine called 'tea'. A great place, and as yet few tourists know about it. A slightly more sophisticated restaurant lies 4km further along: Restaurante La Mata.

Within the next 5km you reach the **Parque Cultural La Zarza**★ (90km). The small, well-equipped museum here (with explanations in English) is well worth a stop. A waymarked path (allow 15-20 minutes each way) heads off behind the museum to two 'caves' (La Zarza and La Zarcita, really rock overhangs), with curious Guanche petroglyphs. The meaning of these spiralled rock carvings has still not been discovered, but it is thought that they have to do with water. *Note* that there is a petrol station 1km past this point, opposite the turn-off to the houses and chapel of San Antonio del Monte.

Continuing west, when you reach the Puntagorda/Garafía junction (⊕ Cruz Roja), turn right. Notice the old *gofio* (maize) mill on the right here. A convoluted road (LP112) down through almond groves brings you to **Garafía** (100.5km ⛪※⊕), another isolated farming outpost, best known for breeding livestock. Reaching the village, turn right for the 16th-century church of Nuestra Señora de la Luz★ shown on page 126, one of the largest on the island. It has an interesting wooden ceiling. Walk 26 begins and ends here … but the truth is that few hikers venture out this far into the 'sticks'. For food there are several local restaurants here, offering good, plain cooking in simple surroundings — among them Santo Domingo in the *plaza* and La Taberna Santi next to the supermarket.

Leaving Garafía, you can make a pleasant circuit by continuing past the square and taking the first right. Then turn right again, to return to the main road. Making for Las Tricias, turn right and follow the road south. Another *gofio* mill appears on the right as you leave Garafía. Once again settlement is sparse. Two more impressive ravines are crossed. Climbing slopes clad with almond trees, you pass through picturesque **Las Tricias**★ (112km), a retreat for 'alternative life-stylers'. Walk 25 would take you right down amongst them all — and past the *gofio* mill shown on pages 122-123. But it's really the great clumps of dragon trees everyone comes to see (photo page 124).

Just 1km above Las Tricias you meet the LP1 signposted back to Garafía. Turn left uphill here, to begin your ascent to the Roque de los Muchachos. After 10km branch off right on the LP4. The ascent gets steeper, the bends sharper. Stunning scenery unravels — over the farmlands of the north, the thickly wooded hillsides, and the sea. Nearer the rim of the crater, the pines vanish and *codeso* (broom) carpets the ground. Pass th first observatory buildings, turn right at the first junction, and head up to the island's highest peak, the **Roque de los Muchachos**★ (145km 📷*i*).

For a spectacular view into the Caldera de Taburiente, walk down to the salient of rock on the right, behind the car park. Over the shoulder of the crater the white-domed buildings of the **Observatorio Astrofísico** glare back at you. This complex, the most important in the northern hemisphere, has many telescopes, including two for the sun and 11 for the furthest galaxies. The Gran Telescopio Canario (installed in 2007) is one of the largest telescopes in the world.

Return to the junction with the LP4 and turn right for Santa Cruz. Rounding the *caldera*, the deep volcanic yellows, oranges and reds in the rock distract you from the panoramic views. Two more *miradores* (**Los Andenes** and **Degollada de Franceses**) on the very edge of the crater (📷) give you another chance to take in this great work of nature. Descending, re-enter the pine zone and after 8km pass the Pico de la Nieve track, starting point for Walk 12 and Short walk 12. Over the pines the east coast begins to open up and, lower down, you get a fine view of Santa Cruz, with a prominent half-crater backdrop. On reaching the LP401, keep left, then turn right on the LP1 into **Santa Cruz** (189km).

Car tour 2: VOLCANIC SPLENDOURS IN THE SOUTH OF LA PALMA

Santa Cruz • Los Canarios (Fuencaliente) • El Paso • La Cumbrecita • El Pilar • Santuario de las Nieves • Santa Cruz

134km/84mi; 5h driving; take the southern exit from Santa Cruz
On route: 🅿 at Las Toscas (Mazo), on the main road above Las Indias, Refugio El Pilar, La Pared Vieja; Picnics (see pages 8-11) 12, 14a-b, (14c); Walks 12-18, (19)
Driving will be slow, due to narrow winding roads. The southern tip of the island can be very windy. **You must book in advance to park at La Cumbrecita: see the final ('reservas purques') website on page 6**

Opening hours
Mazo, market days: 15.00-19.00 Sat; 09.00-13.00 Sun
El Molino (ceramics centre): 09.00-13.00, 15.00-17.00 Mon-Fri
Cueva de Belmaco (archaeological museum) 10.00-15.00 Mon-Sat; tel 922 440090
Bodegas Llanovid: 08.00-14.00 and 15.00-17.00 Mon-Fri
National Park Visitors' Centre: 09.00-18.30 daily, including holidays; tel 922 922280

You'll marvel at the volcanic landscapes on this tour, the kaleidoscope of scenery, and the striking colour contrasts. Gastronomic delights, plain but hearty, lie on route as well — indulge yourself.

Head south on the LP2, passing the long man-made Playa de Bajamar. The turn-off right to the Playa de los Cancajos (⛱▲✕) lies 3km along: with its rock-studded coves, it is the best beach in the vicinity. Just 0.1km further on, turn right (Exit 2b) and, at a roundabout follow signposting for 'Los Canarios'. Beyond the airport turn-off, you head through colourful San Antonio (4.5km ▲✕). Some 1.5km further on, you come to a junction. Continue to the right here, up into the hills (LP206, signposted to 'San José').*

Keep left at both the major junctions you encounter and ignore any turn-offs. The garden plots disappear and the hillsides are overgrown. Entering **Mazo** (12km ⛪▲✕⊕ and Las Toscas 🅿), take the upper road. The market and handicraft centre here are popular with tourists, as is the Corpus Christi festival in June, when flower petals are laid in the streets as pictures and carpets. Mazo, like El Hoyo de Mazo, is a wine-producing area, well known for its strong red wine. Walk 15 ends here.

*But if you are interested in the history of the island, I'd suggest the lower route (LP2, also signposted to 'Los Canarios'). This lower route runs via **El Hoyo de Mazo** (10km ✕). Souvenir hunters may enjoy El Molino, the hillside windmill and ceramics shop on the outskirts of El Hoyo (11km), which was originally an ironmongery. It is beautifully kept,

and in spring the garden is an extravaganza of colour. The artisans here specialise in replicas of the Guanche era. Further on you would pass the Cueva de Belmaco★ (15.5km ⛰M), a large overhang of rock by the roadside with a small archaeological museum. Four rocks on the edge of the overhang are engraved with still-undeciphered petroglyphs.

19

Beyond **Tigalate** (19km), the historians and shoppers rejoin the route at the Mazo/Los Canarios junction. The LP2 takes you across a jagged lava stream, dating from the 1646 eruption of Volcán San Martín (Walk 17). At the 25km-mark a track signposted 'Pino de la Virgen' turns off right to the Fuente de los Roques *zona recreativa*.

Soon the change in scenery is spectacular. Volcanoes begin appearing on the southern tip of the island, where eruptions have dramatically transformed the landscape. Pines are liberally dispersed across the lava, which is covered in reindeer moss. The *cumbre* falls into the sea. Entering the wine-producing village of **Los Canarios** (also known as **Fuencaliente**; 28km ▲✖🅿⊕), where Walk 17 ends and Walk 16 begins, you pass the turn-offs for both the lighthouse (Faro de Fuencaliente) and the volcanoes. The village, the highest on the island, sits on the tail of the *cumbre*, at 680m/2230ft. If you're ready for coffee, try the almond cakes in the Bar La Parada, along to the right.

Return to the first junction in the village and turn right for Las Indias and the volcanoes of San Antonio and Teneguía. This is one of the best grape-growing areas in the Canaries, and soon you will see the large Bodega Teneguía (✖) on your right. It's known for its extensive selection of wines, the most famous being the well-known *malvasia* (malmsey), which has won several international prizes.

Descending into the volcanic world that is the setting for Walk 16, weird and wonderful sights await you. Less than 1km downhill, turn left to the signposted **Volcán de San Antonio**★ (29.5km), shown on pages 90-91. The entrance fee of €5 covers parking and access to the volcano (📷) and visitors' centre (*i*). Thought to be at least 3200 years old, the volcano last erupted

The Volcán de Teneguía: in summer the nearby vineyards are a blaze of brightness in this sombre and windswept landscape.

Car tour 2: Volcanic splendours in the south

in 1677. (See Short walk 16 on page 90 to reach **Roque Teneguía** and the **Volcán de Teneguía**★ from here.)

Continuing towards Las Indias, you have a fine view (☎) onto yellow Roque Teneguía, once a sacred rock, covered with petroglyphs, with the rich blue sea behind it. The jet-black inclines are splashed with lime-green grape vines. Banana plantations lie along the sea flat amidst the lava flows. The village of Los Quemados sits on a pause in the hillside below. Ignore turn-offs to the left. Descending through the sprawling hillside village of **Las Indias** (33km), you look across the southern slopes onto Puerto Naos, with the wall of the *caldera* behind it. At a T-junction with signs for 'La Zamora' and 'El Faro', turn left.*

At the bottom of the road, you weave in and out of banana plantations and pass an impressive hotel complex (▲▲). A pretty inlet follows just over 2km further on. Then a track turns off to the right, to Punta Larga. Out of the banana groves, you head through old and newer lava flows. The newer flow was caused by Teneguía in 1971 and embraces the pretty beach of Playa Echentive (or Playa Nueva; 43.5km). Some 1km further on, turn right for 'El Faro'. Keep right at the fork. (The left fork would take you to some tiny unfrequented coves hidden in the shoreline, worth a visit one day.)

Faro de Fuencaliente (46.5km; photographs pages 2 and 92-93), the out-of-the-way fishermen's retreat where Walk 16 ends, is well worth the visit. There is a small but interesting maritime visitors' centre in the old lighthouse. This is also a good swimming spot, except when a strong south or southwesterly wind is blowing. There is a self-guided trail with information boards in the *salinas* shown on page 2. Right in the middle of these salt pans is a themed restaurant, 'Jardin de la Sal' (✕), with excellent views and equally great food. Salt from the *salinas* can be bought in a little shop next to it.

Return to the road and turn right. The deep red-tinted Volcán de Teneguía catches your attention as you ascend into volcanic mounds. Climb steeply through the fresh lava streams of Teneguía and pass through the apron of vineyards that encircle the village of Los Canarios (57km). Back on the LP2, turn left, go through the village and soon pass two roadside picnic areas (⛱) overlooking the coast — one to the right and one to the left. Half a kilometre past the second picnic area lies the **Mirador de las Indias** (☎), from where you have an excellent view

---

*Or first take a 3km return detour to the *right*, to the pretty little cove of Playa de Zamora. Some 200m past the signposted lane down to the parking area for the *kiosko*, you'll see a path descending to Playa de Zamora, a cove set at the foot of high cliffs. Please don't sit directly below the cliffs, as there is often rockfall. Several rocky islets sit offshore, and the coastline has pinkish cliffs. Just above Playa de Zamora is one of the few *kioskos* left on the coast, serving up good fish and great views (many of these 'sheds', some illegally built, but all full of 'local colour', were closed down by the authorities in recent years).

The Ermita de la Virgen del Pino, with its grand old pine (Walks 12 and 13)

back over terraced vineyards and the village of the same name. The road climbs to 800m/2625ft, with marvellous sea views. At 64km **El Charco**, another *mirador* (📷), affords fine views across the cliffs, over to Puerto Naos. Beyond a shady pine wood, you overlook great spewings of lava from eruptions in the 18th century. The picturesque village of **Jedey** sits amidst this turmoil. **Las Manchas**, an area of viticulture, follows. Then you come to one of the most popular bodegas on the island, Bodegón/Restaurant Tamanca (72km ✕), a cave cut into the hillside. At the very least try some cheese and ham with a tipple! You'll see the mounted head of a *mouflon* (barbary sheep) in the bar: a few still roam the heights of the *caldera*.

The village of **San Nicolás** lies just around the bend. During the volcanic eruption of 1949, San Nicolás was in the path of a descending lava flow. The people prayed together to save their village, and the flow changed course. It encircled the village, but then continued below it. A shrine commemorates this miracle.

Remain on the LP2 beyond San Nicolás. Settlement slowly creeps over the sloping plain. On reaching the Los Canarios/Los Llanos junction, at **Tajuya** (76km ✕), turn right uphill on the LP3 to El Paso. The towering crater walls are the focal point in the landscape. **El Paso** (79km 🛆🏠✕🚍⊕) sprawls amidst the gardens, orchards, and almond fields that cover the floor of a high open valley. This village is a favourite with expatriates.

Some 3km above El Paso, at the second roundabout, turn left on the LP302 for the Parque Nacional. Stop at the parking area on the right for the National Park Information Centre (*i*), to pick up a free admission ticket for your next stop, the Cumbrecita (no ticket is needed after 16.00). Pass through the first junction (where a right turn leads to the Ermita de la Virgen del Pino and the grand pine shown above; Picnic 12, Walk 12), then keep right at the next junction for La Cumbrecita. (Keeping straight on here would take you to the starting point for Walk 19 which climbs Pico Bejenado.) From **La Cumbrecita** (89km 📷), starting point for Walk 13, you enjoy a splendid view over the Caldera de Taburiente, a massive cauldron filled with jagged blades of tumbling ridges.

Return to the LP3 and turn

Car tour 2: Volcanic splendours in the south

left. After 3km turn right on the LP301 for the El Pilar Zona Recreativa and climb steadily, in an appealing landscape of coal-black slopes and pine forest. You pass a track off right 4km uphill: it leads to the small volcanic 'desert' shown on pages 84-85, the **Llano del Jable** (☞; Picnic 14c, Walk 14). About 1km further on, where a track heads south, is the eponymous *mirador*, with fine views over the volcanic plains you just passed and up to Los Llanos in the distance. Just before crossing the *cumbre*, you pass the **Refugio El Pilar** (106km △🎪; Picnic 14b, Walks 12, 14, 15 and 17), a popular picnic and camping area in a pine forest. Just above it, to the left, is the Cumbre Nueva track that is followed in Alternative walk 12-2.

On the other side of the *cumbre* the vegetation changes from pines to laurel forest. A dark green carpet of dense woods stretches across the eastern escarpment. This fine view reaches as far as Puntallana. On clear days El Teide can be seen above the foaming white clouds that separate La Palma and Tenerife (☞ at 109km). Some 1.5km below the viewpoint lies **La Pared Vieja** (🎪; Picnic 14a, Walk 14), a picnic area in laurel woods.

Returning to civilization, you enter the farming village of **San Isidro** (118km), which enjoys an expansive panorama along the wall of the *cumbre* and over the twin villages of San Pedro and San José. San Isidro is known for its cattle market, held in May. Continuing downhill, soon you'll spot a large dragon tree below the road, off a sharp bend — actually two trees, intertwined (**Los Dragos Gemelos★**; the 'twins'). Reaching the LP202, head left into **San Pedro** (also known as Breña Alta; 123km ♦✕🍽) in the midst of a tobacco-growing area. A farmer's market is held here each Saturday morning. Circle the *plaza*, remaining on the LP202. At the next important junction, cross over the LP3, to continue towards the 'Santuario de las Nieves'. But first turn off right at the roundabout just ahead, to the **Mirador de la Concepción** (☞), the perfect spot from which to view Santa Cruz. Back at the roundabout, the beautiful red building is the restaurant Casa Osmunda (✕), with Palmerian *'nouvelle cuisine'* — quite a novelty on the island. Keep straight on at the roundabout. You pass the restaurant Chipi Chipi, on the left. Housed in cabanas in a courtyard crammed with greenery, it is reasonably priced and always packed.

Rounding a bend, you look across a ravine sprinkled with palms to the tree-shaded **Santuario de las Nieves★** (129km ✝M), strikingly set in a rocky ridge. To reach the sanctuary, turn right at the roundabout. The church (16C) houses a 15th-century terracotta statue of the island's patron saint, Our Lady of the Snows. Her festival is celebrated annually on the fifth of August. But every five years a month-long fiesta takes place (the 'Bajada de la Virgen'), when the statue is carried down into Santa Cruz. It draws tens of thousands of pilgrims and tourists.

Drive down from the church back onto the LP101 and, following signs for Santa Cruz, take the second turning to the right. A very steep, winding descent takes you back to **Santa Cruz** far below (134km).

3: CALDERA DE TABURIENTE

...s • Caldera de Taburiente • Barranco de las ... • Los Brecitos • Tazacorte • Mirador El Time • ...rda) • Los Llanos

57km/36mi; 3-4h driving. See also large-scale map on pages 106-107.
On route: Picnic (see pages 8-11) 21; Walks 20-22. (Walks 23 and 24 and the El Fayal picnic site (⊼) are on the Puntagorda detour route.)
Drive carefully: although the road up to Los Brecitos is tarmac, it is very narrow and vertiginous. You are not allowed to stop on the road, and there is limited turn-around space. Parking is not allowed at Los Brecitos, and you may be turned back by a park warden if there are too many cars on the road. The best solution is to drive only as far as the Barranco de las Angustias, the floor of the crater, and then take one of the shuttle jeep or van taxis up to Los Brecitos (these only operate from 08.30 until about 12.30); the shared cost is about €12-13 per person.

All visitors to La Palma should spend at least one day in the magnificent Caldera de Taburiente. This short tour is designed to be combined with Walk 21, as a half-day tour, half-day hike.

Leaving from **Los Llanos** (✝🏨▲✕🅿⊕), turn north on Avenida Doctor Fleming and turn right at the T-junction. The road curves round to the left: go through an intersection and follow signs for 'La Caldera', keeping right at the first fork and left at the second. Climb to the edge of the Barranco de las Angustias and, at a T-junction, turn right to descend into the **Caldera de Taburiente★**.

Car tour 3: Caldera de Taburiente   25

Some 5km along you're in the bed of the dramatic **Barranco de las Angustias** (Picnic 21). If there are not too many tourists about, and the park wardens don't turn you back, you may be able to take your car further up the road. Otherwise I highly recommend sharing a jeep taxi up to **Los Brecitos** (16km 🚖). Whether with your own wheels or by jeep taxi, the 11km climb of almost 1000m/3300ft, will take you through mountain scenery unequalled on the island. On your return, *do* follow at least part of Walk 21 to make the most of your visit; see notes on page 110.

From the *caldera* retrace your route to **Los Llanos** (32km) and turn right on the main LP2. Some 2km downhill, follow the LP2 left to **Tazacorte** (39.5km ▲♦✕🅿⊕), buried amidst the banana plantations that cover these slopes. Continue through the village to **Puerto de Tazacorte** (40km ♦✕), a colourful and fashionable seaside village with lovely restaurants lining the boulevard beside the beach. From here ascend the canyon-sized Barranco de las Angustias again in the setting shown on pages 112-113.

Joining the LP1, continue left uphill to the **Mirador El Time** (47.5km 🚖✕), the climax of one of the island's most exhilarating routes. The impressive *barranco* plunges 500m/1650ft directly below you here, and your view fans out over the banana plantations that fill the extensive Los Llanos valley, to the *cumbre*, and along the volcano-dented southern spine. Walk 22 winds its way down these sheer cliffs to Puerto de Tazacorte; it makes an excellent late afternoon walk.

Suggested detour, 32km return: If you have time, consider going on to Puntagorda via Tijarafe (✕🅿⊕) and Tinizara (✕). Tijarafe's Walk 23, which will turn your legs to jelly, is a must for the fit. Walk 24 is a gentler roller-coaster hike, from Tijarafe to Tinizara. At Puntagorda there is the El Fayal picnic site and a nearby indoor market selling local foods and handicrafts (weekends only)

Otherwise, pour yourself a glass of the local wine, put your feet up, and take in an 'El Time sunset', before heading back the 9.5km along the LP1 to **Los Llanos** (57km).

Heading up the Barranco de las Angustias, through a landscape of banana groves

Car tour 4: EL HIERRO — HIGHLIGHTS

Tigaday • Sabinosa • La Dehesa • (Faro de Orchilla) • Cruz de los Reyes • Hoya del Morcillo • El Pinar • Cala de Tacorón • Mirador de las Playas • Mirador de Jinama • Mirador de la Peña • Mocanal • Pozo de las Calcosas • Valverde • San Andrés • Tigaday

184km/115mi; 5h driving; start out from Tigaday.
On route: ⛽ at Playa del Verodal, (Puerto de Orchilla), Hoya del Morcillo, Cala de Tacorón, (Charco Manso, Las Playas); Picnics (see pages 8-11) 30a-b, 32, 34; Walks 27-35

This tour follows roads of all kinds. Some 25km is on gravel (not recommended immediately after wet weather, due to rockfall). The detour to the Faro de Orchilla takes in an extra 10km of sometimes rough road (in winter or after heavy rain only suitable for four wheel drive vehicles). There are two narrow stretches of road without guard rails which some motorists may find unnerving: on the ascent up the cumbre beyond the turn-off to Playa del Verodal, and on the road to Cala de Tacorón in the south. Note that visibility on the cumbre can be zero, due to low clouds and mist. Always be alert for foraging animals. Petrol is only available at Taibique (near El Pinar), Tigaday and Valverde (some stations will be closed in the afternoon on Sundays and holidays). All the roads are generally narrow and winding, so drive slowly.

Opening hours
Eco-museo de Guinea and Lagartario (plus an interesting cave): open daily all year from 10.00-18.00, but closed on Sundays and Mondays in winter

The diversity of landscapes encountered on this tiny island will leave you spellbound. There are vast open tracts of lava, fields of craters, herbaceous highlands, spacious forests of towering pines, small boskets of laurel, and inviting rock pools. If you're rushed for time, then keep to the main tour, but if you're on the island for a few days, then *do* try to take all the suggested detours.

Tigaday is the starting point for the drive. For those of you staying elsewhere, recommended sights in the vicinity are the Eco-museo de Guinea, a restored hamlet, and the nearby Lagartario which houses the large Salmor lizards (both on the road to Las Puntas); the Embarcadero de Punta Grande (if only to see the smallest hotel in the world!); and the bell-tower of Frontera's church, which crowns a rust-red volcanic hill above the church itself. The hilltop, shown opposite, is the perfect spot to take in a sunset.

Set out from **Frontera/Tigaday** (✝🏔️🏔️🏔️✖️🅿️⊕) by heading west towards Sabinosa on the HI50. You pass through a string of villages (✖️) set on the steep rocky volcanic slopes that roll down off the *cumbre*. Fig trees and vineyards grow out of the *malpais* that coats the slopes (try the fine local wine). Rounding a hillside, you overlook **Sabinosa** (8km 🏔️✖️), the village shown on page 131. Stark and severe, this whitewashed settlement is the island's prize — superbly sited on volcanic slopes at the foot of the wooded central

26

Looking across Tigaday and Frontera to the wall of the El Golfo crater. The bell-tower of Frontera's church (Virgen de la Candelaria) stands apart on a rust-red hilltop. Walks 30 and 31 ascend the wooded slopes at the right of the photo.

spine of mountains. Walk 27 ends here, and Walk 28 is a circuit based on Sabinosa. Terraced vineyards ladder the surrounding hillsides.

A narrow winding road takes you down to the health spa of **Pozo de la Salud★** (12km ▰▴✕🏨), known for the reputedly curative powers of its sulphur and radium spring. This one-horse hamlet enjoys a superb backdrop. From the pretty, manicured *mirador* below the hotel you can look along the low craggy sea cliffs into a viridescent sea. Drink some of the salty spring water from the little well in the rock here, where the sheer *cumbre* walls provide a magnificent backdrop; the scenery alone has curative powers!

Continuing further west, you enter the island's most striking and isolated corner, where an extravaganza of volcanic scenery awaits you. Explore it on foot: I *highly recommend* easy Walk 29 for everyone: stop at the parking area (14.6km) for **Arenas Blancas**, a tiny patch of golden yellow sand set in the lava coastline.

Disappearing into *malpais* again, stabs of rich volcanic reds and orange-tinted rust-brown hues catch your attention. Your next turn-off comes up at 17.5km: turn sharp right for 'Playa del Verodal'. Then, 100m further on, where the asphalt ends, turn right on a good track. The red sandy beach of **Playa del Verodal** (18.5km 🅿) is a pretty, but windy spot, with a dramatic backdrop of maroon-tinted cliffs. *Beware:* the sea can be rough here!

Back on the main road, turn right. Ascending steeply, superb views over the coastal lava shelf

27

unfold behind you. The landscape is barren and rocky; xerophytic vegetation grows out of the rock. This part of the island is known as **La Dehesa**.

Suggested detour: After 27km you reach the signposted turn-off right for the 'Faro de Orchilla'. The first 2km is partly asphalted, then you turn left on a motorable track (in winter or after heavy rain only suitable for 4WD). Descending to the lighthouse, you enter a world of volcanic cones and lava streams and look down over a jagged, lava-encrusted point of land. Massive *Euphorbias* grow out of the lava here. Red-tinted craters come out of hiding. Approaching the lighthouse, you pass a heavily signposted fork leading left to tiny Puerto de Orchilla (⌂), where it's possible to swim. Until 1844, the **Faro de Orchilla**★ (📷) was 'the edge of the world': before it was repositioned at Greenwich, 0° of longitude was located here at the western edge of El Hierro. Amble along the impressive sea cliffs behind the building. Then return to the main road and turn right.

The main tour bypasses the Orchilla turn-off. You drive over two cattle-grids and, at the junction that follows, turn left for the 'Mirador del Basco' and 'El Sabinar', soon coming to the **Ermita de la Virgen de los Reyes**★ (30.5km ❀; Walk 17). This dazzling-white, isolated refuge, shown on pages 132-133, is the sanctuary of the island's patron saint. Every four years, on the first weekend in July, a very popular pilgrimage (the 'Bajada de la Virgen') begins here, and an image of the Madonna crosses the island to Valverde. (The island's most famous walk, the 28km-long 'Camino de la Virgin', follows this pilgrimage route, and some of our walks use the trail from time to time.) The fiesta continues for almost a month.

Half a kilometre further on the way reverts to a rutted gravel road. At a signposted junction, turn left. Another cattle-grid is encountered, and again the countryside changes. Undulating pastures criss-crossed with stone walls stretch back up to the hills. Remaining on the main metalled road, take the first turn-off left and wind your way down to **El Sabinar**★ (34.5km), a magnificent refuge for scatterings of centuries-old, twisted and gnarled *sabinas* (native junipers) — the result of the harsh unrelenting winds that batter this corner of the island. Less than 1km downhill, the track ends just in front of the island's most famous and most photographed specimen (see page 1). An interesting information board explains the origin of these weird, 'arthritic' trees — unique in the archipelago. The surrounding vegetation here is thickly covered in moss and lichen. Please note that this is a protected area.

Return to the junction and turn left. Further north along the gravel road, you meet a fork: keep right for the *mirador,* driving through fragments of pine woods — a picturesque corner in this inhospitable area. The **Mirador del Basco** (36.5km 📷) sits high on the very edge of the escarpment that encircles El Golfo. The stunning panorama extends all across the gulf, with Pozo de la Salud immediately below you. Walk 28 climbs to El Sabinar via this viewpoint.

Returning to the junction just before the *ermita* (41km), go straight on for 'Valverde' and 'El Pinar'. A meandering ascent takes

Eco-museo at Guinea near Tigaday — a restored old village

you up to the island's cloud-swept heights. Pines patch the gravelly slopes. Pass the turn-off right for El Julán and Hoya del Morcillo, and keep left, now on a gravel road. Volcanic hues of maroon, pink, and yellow stain the hillsides. High on the *cumbre*, your view stretches over the pines to the sea and then to the treeless southern tip of La Restinga. You pass below El Hierro's highest summit, Malpaso (1500m/4920ft): but for the signpost, you would never notice it.

A simple wooden cross and concrete altar by the side of the road mark **Cruz de los Reyes** (56.5km), the pilgrims' rest stop en route to Valverde from the Ermita de la Virgen de los Reyes. On a sealed road once again, you look out over the low wooded hills of El Pinar, your next destination. Coming to the Frontera/Valverde junction (starting point for Walks 32, 34 and 35), keep right along the HI1, immediately passing the signposted path to the **Mirador de la Llanía** (📷; Picnic 32). Some 0.4km further on, turn right for 'Hoya del Morcillo, El Pinar, La Restinga'. Briefly disappearing into laurel woods, the road winds down towards El Pinar, passing through El Hierro's majestic Canary pine wood (see page 36), where centuries-old pines with massive girths leave you in awe. Just under 4km downhill, keep right. Follow this up with a left turn into the large picnic area of **Hoya del Morcillo** (64.5km △🎋), set in the middle of the forest. Return to the main road and turn right for 'El Pinar' and 'La Restinga'. At the T-junction that follows, turn right again. The nearby slopes are sprinkled with almond trees.

Entering **El Pinar**, which comprises the villages of **Las Casas** and **Taibique**, take the first right turn (signposted 'Tanajara'), where the main road curves left. Keep straight through a junction, then turn right at the next junction and ascend a narrow road up to the **Mirador Tanajara** (69km 📷). If you're game, climb the wooden viewing platform for a good view over the sprawling villages of Las Casas and Taibique. The fields are scattered with large umbrella-shaped fig trees, and almond, apricot and pear trees abound, as do small vineyards. To the south lies a chain of volcanic craters. Back on the main road, turn right for 'El Pinar' and 'Restinga' and descend to **Taibique** (72.5km ⛺▲✕🚻⊕M). The village is known for handicrafts: weaving, woodcarving and basketry.

Out of the village, you descend south through a curious landscape of ropey lava and block lava. Less than 10km below El Pinar, just past a Volcano Visitors' Centre★ on the left, turn off right for 'Cala de Tacorón'. Descending into a striking sea view across the western

Sea pools (charcos) *at Cala de Tacorón*

wing of the island, the road twists its way down a sheer slope to a lava platform jutting out into the sea. **Cala de Tacorón** (87km ⌂) is a quiet, out-of-the-way spot with superb *charcos* (sea pools) for swimmers, mouth-watering scenery, and a lovely little bar that serves food. With the south's more reliable sunshine, this is the place to come for your beach day. I think it beats La Restinga hands down. The main tour in fact bypasses La Restinga (♦✕), by turning left at the Tacorón junction, heading straight back to El Pinar. (La Restinga, small fishing village-cum-resort, 7km to the south, has an attractive port, good fish restaurants, and a visitors' centre.)

From **El Pinar** keep straight uphill past the El Morcillo junction, then turn off right to the **Mirador de las Playas** (109.5km ⌂; Walk 34). From the edge of a 1000m/3300ft-high bluff, you look straight down onto the severe but breathtakingly beautiful *playas* — the setting shown in the photograph on page 150.

Back on the main road, head right. The hillsides are covered in *tagasaste*, a shrub grown for animal fodder. Climbing to a tableland, the **Meseta de Nisdafe**, you reach the roof of the island, home of the best pastures, where cows and sheep graze. San Andrés is the small village over on the right, encircling the base of a small volcanic cone. When you rejoin the H1, keep left and, 2km along, turn right to the **Mirador de Jinama** (117.5km ⌂; Picnic 30a, Walks 30 and 31) where, from the top of the *cumbre*, your view stretches the length of El Golfo to the west.

Continuing northeast on a narrow country road, bump your way across the plateau, lost amidst the myriad of stone walls that divide it up into tiny squares. When a farmer dies on El Hierro, his fields are always divided up among all his children, each of whom partitions his or her share. And so the fields get smaller, while the walls increase. Small cinder cones cover the plateau.

You descend to the H10, where you turn left downhill for 2km to the **Mirador de la Peña**★ (124.5km ⌂✕; Picnic 30b, Walk 30). Lanzarote's César Manrique was the creator of this superbly-sited restaurant/bar, which claims the island's best view of El Golfo. These cliffs were the habitat of a very rare lizard, the *lagarto de salmor*, which supposedly reaches a length of 70cm/28in. (*Do* visit the Lagartario at the Eco-museo de Guinea!)

Continuing north through fertile farmlands and the hamlets of **Guarazoca** and **Erese**, dense xerophytic vegetation cloaks the rocky inclines. The traditional stone dwellings are hardly noticeable in this backdrop. Entering

Car tour 4: El Hierro — highlights 31

Mocanal (128km), the most picturesque village on the island, take the first turn-off left (along the old road). This narrow road squeezes past a string of charming old houses, where window and door frames all vary in colour.

Just over 1km along, at a signposted, slightly larger junction, turn left for 'Pozo de las Calcosas'. A steep winding descent follows. The slopes ease out as they roll seawards. *Vinagrera* (of the dock family) proliferates here and provides a source of food for the many goats. ('Calcosas' is the local name for *vinagrera*.) At the next junction, go straight on to **Pozo de las Calcosas★** (133.5km ▲✕▣), which at first appears to be an unexciting hamlet set back off the sea cliffs. However, on the rocky shore at the foot of these bluffs sits a century-old, once-deserted fishing hamlet which has been beautifully restored. Steps lead down to this appealing huddle of stone houses and the nearby natural rock pool. The restaurants above the *mirador* here serve excellent fresh seafood.

At the junction above Pozo de las Calcosas, turn left to **Echedo** (138.5km ✕), a wine- and fruit-producing village boasting the best climate on the island. Entering the village, ignore a turning to the right, but turn right at the T-junction that follows. (A left turn at this T-junction would take you to the brilliant blue sea pools of Charco Manso, 4km away; ⊟.) Surrounded by rocky hills and scattered amidst the now-familiar stone walls, Echedo is a charmer. Ascending to Valverde, you overlook the black and brown slopes of Montaña Tanagiscaba. When you meet the main road, turn left.

After just 100m you're at the **Mirador de las Pernadas** (▣), from where there is a fine view over the tiny seaside resort of Tamaduste. Then you come to a junction on the outskirts of **Valverde** (142km ╬▲▲▲✕⊟⊕M). This small, rather plain rural town, sitting at an altitude of 700m, is the island's capital ... known as the 'London of the Canaries, because it is so often shrouded in fog.) Turn right and pass through the town.

Suggested detours: If you are on the island for a while, you may wish to visit the seaside resort of **Tamaduste** (▲✕), 8km north of the capital via the airport road, or take the very scenic coastal route from **Puerto de la Estaca** (two ⊟) to the *parador* (▲✕), 18km southeast of Valverde.

Leave Valverde on the H11. Bypassing Tiñor, you climb above steep, rocky, xerophyte-clad slopes to the small traditional farming village of **San Andrés** (✕). At an altitude of 1100m, this is El Hierro's highest village. (The turn-off to Isora, just before San Andrés, leads to the Mirador de Isora, another spectacular lookout point over Las Playas. Walk 35 makes a fairly hair-raising descent down the sheer escarpment that tumbles away below this *mirador*.) The famous 'Arbol Santo' worshipped by the bimbaches (El Hierro's original inhabitants) and shown on pages 128-129 is not far from San Andrés; Walk 33 would take you to it.

Go straight through both junctions just outside San Andrés, and once again weave your way through the maze of stone walls, following the H11 — the spectacular, but long and winding old road through the laurel forest — back to **Tigaday** (175km).

Walking

La Palma and El Hierro offer unlimited scope for walkers. This book covers a good cross-section of walks on both islands. Due to the rugged, mountainous terrain of these islands, many of the walks in the book are quite strenuous, but I usually suggest a less difficult alternative — perhaps a short walk, or just a stroll to a picnic spot.

I hope you will also make up your own walk combinations. I've shown where my routes link up on the walking maps, and the fold-out touring map shows the general location of all the walks. But only join up walks by using routes described in this guide or the officially waymarked trails. 'Official' trails are very well signposted, so even if the trail is not described in detail in my notes, you can still use them with confidence to short-cut (or 'long-cut') any of my walks.

There are walks in this book for everyone.

Beginners: Start on the walks graded 'easy', and be sure to look at any short or alternative walks — some are easy versions of the long hikes. You need look no further than the picnic suggestions on pages 8 to 11 to find a large selection of *very* easy rambles.

Experienced walkers: If you are used to rough terrain and have a head for heights, you should be able to tackle all the walks in the book, *except those colour-coded black* (see opposite). Of course, you must take into account the season and weather conditions. For example, in rainy weather some of the *barranco* walks will be unsuitable; in strong winds or snow do not plan excursions to the mountains! And always remember that **storm damage can make these routes unsafe at any time!** Remember, too: always follow the route as described in this book. If you have not reached one of the landmarks after a reasonable time, you must go back to the last 'sure' point and start again.

All walkers: *Do* check the update service described on the inside front cover of the book before you travel!

Grading, waymarking, maps, GPS

There is a quick overview of each walk's **grade** in the Contents. But in the limited space we've only had room to show the ***lowest grade of a main walk:*** for full details of grading, see the introductory remarks about the walk itself.

Walking

Below is a brief overview of the three gradings:

● easy-moderate — ascents/descents of no more than about 300-500m/1000-1800ft; good surfaces underfoot; easily followed

● moderate-strenuous — ascents/descents may be over 500m/1800ft; variable surfaces underfoot — you must be sure-footed and agile; possible route-finding problems in poor visibility

● expert — only suitable for very experienced hillwalkers with a head for heights; hazards may include landslides or balancing on the narrow ledges with no respite from constant exposure

Any of the above grades may, if applicable, be followed by:

❗ *danger* of vertigo — you must have a *very* good head for heights

Waymarking and **signposting** have been brought up to 'Euro' standards on most routes. There are three types of waymarking:

■ *Red and white* waymarks indicating GR routes ('Grandes Recorridos': long-distance footpaths);
■ *Yellow and white* waymarks indicating PR routes ('Pequeños Recorridos': short trails of up to six hours);
■ *Green and white* waymarks indicating SL routes ('Senderos Locales': local trails, up to about 10km long).
■ For all these routes, two parallel stripes mean 'continue this way'; right-angled stripes indicate a 'change of direction'; an 'X' means 'wrong way'.

Walkers' signposts on the Ruta de los Volcanes: the top fingerpost marks a route shared by the GR131 (red and white) and an SL trail (green and white); the middle fingerpost is solely for the GR131 and the bottom one for the SL VM 125 trail. If one of the trails were an 'LP' route, the equivalent part of the sign would be yellow. But you will also find fingerposts with no colour at all, or handwritten, or carved in wood.

Our walking maps include official trails adjacent to our walks, with their relevant numbers printed in purple. This should give you ample scope for devising even more walks — perhaps a linear route to catch a bus or a circuit back to your car. For full details of waymarked walks on **La Palma**, see www.senderosdelapalma.es; the site lists all the island's official routes. They also publish a 'topoguide' of some 350 pages, which can be bought at various tourist offices. For **El Hierro** see www.senderosdelhierro.com, for an interactive map. You can also download KLM files for viewing in Google Earth or for reformatting to GPX.

The **maps** in this book are based on Openstreetmap mapping (see page 2), but have been very heavily annotated from notes and GPS work in the field. It is a pity that we have to reproduce them at only 1:50,000 (with just a few at 1:25,000) to keep the book to a manageable size; quite a few walkers buy both the paperback *and* our downloadable pdf files so that they can print the maps at a larger size — or you can enlarge them on a photocopier.

Free **GPS tracks** are available for all my walks: see the La Palma page on the Sunflower website. Please bear in mind, however, that GPS readings should *never* be relied upon as your sole reference point. Conditions can change at any time — especially in the Canaries, where mountainsides can come down overnight. And even if you cannot be bothered to use GPS on the ground, you may nevertheless enjoy opening the GPX files in Google Earth to preview the walks in advance!

Where to stay

There are two main resorts on **La Palma**: Los Cancajos on the eastern side of the island and Puerto Naos in the west. There is also a large Princess chain hotel in Fuencaliente near the coast. All are fairly well served by public transport. But I would recommend Santa Cruz or Los Llanos over any of these resorts, both for atmosphere and for getting to and from walks by public transport.

If you have a hire car, however, the island's your oyster — and you might choose to rent one of the *casas rurales* (charming old country houses converted into tourist accommodation). They are reasonably priced and often superbly located. *I highly recommend them.* For information, contact the Asociación de Turismo Rural (tel: 922-430625) or see www.islabonita.com.

The main tourist centres on **El Hierro** are Tigaday/Frontera and La Restinga. Tigaday is my choice, but La Restinga boasts more sunshine. Although bus services on the island have increased somewhat, you really *do* need to rent a car to make the best of El Hierro.

Both La Palma and El Hierro have **government-run hotels** *(paradores)*. El Hierro's is magnificently sited (see photograph on page 153), but well off the beaten track. Independent travellers should always book their accommodation a few nights in advance — in the peak season (Christmas through Easter), at least a month in advance!

What to take

Please don't attempt the more difficult walks in this book without the proper gear. For each walk, the *minimum year-round equipment* is listed. Where walking boots are required, there is no substitute: you will need to rely on the grip and ankle support they provide, as well as their waterproof qualities. All other walks should be done with stout lace-up shoes with thick rubber soles, to grip on wet, slippery surfaces.

You may find the following packing list useful:

- walking boots, spare bootlaces
- mobile/smartphone/gps
- waterproof rain gear (outside summer months)
- long-sleeved shirt (sun protection)
- first-aid kit, including bandages
- walking pole(s)
- windproof (zip opening)
- trail map(s) (see page 33)
- extra pair of socks
- sunhat, sunglasses, suncream
- up-to-date bus timetable
- small rucksack
- plastic bottle with water-purifying tablets
- long trousers, tight at the ankles
- insect repellent
- knives and openers
- lightweight fleece, warm fleece
- swimming things
- groundsheet
- torch, whistle, compass

Please bear in mind that I've not done *every* walk in this book under *all* weather conditions. Use good judgement to modify my lists according to the season.

Weather

The average yearly temperature on both islands is 20°C — perfect for hiking. Three chief winds determine the weather on both islands. The **trade wind** (*el alisio*) comes from the **northeast** with speeds of anything up to 25km/h. Its low, fluffy clouds hover over the north for much of the year, lying at a height of 600-1500m (2000-5000ft). They bring lots of moisture and so keep the islands green. However, the southern sides of the islands are much drier and hotter. The *tiempo sur* is an **southerly** wind which originates over the Sahara and brings hot weather, usually accompanied by fine dust particles. Between November and March, **northwesterly and southwesterly** winds may blow in with storms. Seldom will this ruin an entire day, *but never venture into the mountains when a strong wind is blowing from the west; it's far too dangerous, as it could bring tremendous rainfall within a short time!*

Dogs — and other nuisances

The few **dogs** you'll encounter are mostly all bark, no bite. But if dogs worry you, you might like to invest in a 'Dog Dazer' — an ultrasonic device which persuades aggressive

36   Landscapes of La Palma and El Hierro

dogs to back off without harming them. These are available from Sunflower Books: contact them for more information (www.sunflowerbooks.co.uk).

Ticks *are* a nuisance: they're prevalent in spring. Keep arms and legs covered, and the problem is solved. On El Hierro, if you're crossing pastures, give **billy goats** a wide berth, and make sure there's a wall/fence between you and the **bulls**! During the hunting season (August to December), **hunters** blasting away may frighten you. Exercise your lungs if you think they're too close. Neither island has any snakes. Although rarely encountered, black widow **spiders** exist on both islands, and also red or black **centipedes**, which also have a dangerous sting.

The majestic Canary pine plays a very important ecological role. The prevailing northeasterly trade winds carry clouds to the northern slopes and create an atmosphere which causes condensation. The drippings from this moisture were measured over the period of a year and yielded an incredible 2000 litres per square metre! This may not mean much to you — until I tell you that a reasonable rainfall for a year yields about 500 litres per square metre. This is the reason for the continuous planting of trees in bare or denuded areas of the forest: to feed the underground reservoirs, the galerías. *From these* galerías *(tunnels), water is piped to all parts of the island. La Palma relies heavily on these water sources, because there are no natural wells and few streams with a permanent flow of water. Walk 13 is a good introduction to La Palma's* galerías *— we pass several of them! At the right is the old water station by the Galería de Tabercorade, not far into the walk. At the left is a* galería *proper — a water tunnel pierced in the rock wall.*

Country code

A code for behaviour is very important on these islands, where the rugged terrain can lead to dangerous mistakes.

- **Only light fires** at picnic areas with fireplaces.
- **Do not frighten animals.**
- **Walk quietly** through all hamlets and villages, and take care not to provoke the dogs.
- **Protect all wild and cultivated plants.** Obviously fruit and other crops are someone's private property.
- **Leave all gates just as you found them**.
- **Never walk over cultivated land.**
- **Take your litter away with you.**

Advice for walkers

The following points cannot be stressed too often:

- **At any time a walk may become unsafe** due to storm damage or bulldozing. If the route is not as described in this book, and your way ahead is not secure, do not go on.
- **Walks graded black (●) for experts** may be unsuitable for winter, and all mountain walks may be hazardous then.
- **Never walk alone** and *always* tell a responsible person *exactly* where you are going and what time you plan to return. If you become lost or injure yourself, it may be a long time before you are found. Four is the best walking group: if someone is injured, two can go for help.
- **Do not overestimate your energies** — your speed will be determined by the slowest walker in your group.
- **Transport connections** at the end of a walk may be vital.
- **Proper shoes or boots** are a necessity.
- **Mists** can suddenly appear on the higher elevations.
- **Warm clothing** is needed in the mountains; even in summer take some along, in case you are delayed.
- **Extra rations** must be taken on long walks.
- **Mobile or smartphone, compass, whistle, torch, first-aid kit** weigh little, but might save your life.
- **Always take a sunhat with you**, and in summer a cover-up for your arms and legs as well.
- **A stout stick/walking pole** is a help on rough terrain and to discourage the rare unfriendly dog.
- *Do not take risks!* Some of the walks cross remote country and can be ***very cold and potentially hazardous.*** Distances here can be deceptive, perhaps with exhausting descents into and ascents out of hidden *barrancos* between you and your goal. Only link up walks by following routes on the walking maps; don't attempt to cross unmapped terrain.

Spanish for walkers

In the tourist centres many people speak English. But once out in the countryside, a few words of Spanish will be helpful, especially if you lose your way. Here's a way to communicate in Spanish that is (almost) foolproof. First, memorise the few short key questions and their possible answers below. Then, when you have your 'mini-speech' memorised, always ask the many questions you can concoct from it **in such a way that you get a 'sí' (yes) or 'no' answer**. Never ask an open-ended question like 'Where is the main road?' Instead, ask the question and then *suggest the most likely answer yourself*. For instance: 'Good day, sir. Please — where is the path to Mazo? *Is it straight ahead?*' Now, unless you get a '*sí*' response, try: '*Is it to the left?*' If you go through the list of answers to your own question, you should eventually get a '*sí*' response — probably with a vigorous nod of the head — and this is more reassuring than relying solely on sign language.

Following are the two most likely situations in which you may have to practice some Spanish. The dots (...) show where you will fill in the name of your destination. Approximate pronunciation of place names is in the Index.

- **Asking the way**

The key questions

English	*Spanish*	*pronounced as*
Good day,	Buenos días	**Boo**-eh-nos **dee**-ahs
sir (madam, miss).	señor (señora, señorita).	sen-**yor** (sen-**yor**-ah sen-yor-**ee**-tah).
Please — where is	Por favor — dónde está	**Poor** fah-**voor** — **dohn**-day es-**tah**
the road to ... ?	la carretera a ...?	la cah-reh-**teh**-rah ah ...?
the footpath to ...?	la senda de ...?	lah **sen**-dah day ...?
the way to ...?	el camino a ...?	el cah-**mee**-noh ah ...?
the bus stop?	la parada?	lah par-**rah**-dah?
Many thanks.	Muchas gracias.	**Moo**-chas **gra**-thee-as.

Possible answers

English	*Spanish*	*pronounced as*
is it here?	está aquí?	es-**tah** ah-**kee**?
straight ahead?	todo recto?	**toh**-doh **rec**-toh?
behind?	detrás?	day-**tras**?
to the right?	a la derecha?	ah lah day-**reh**-chah?
to the left?	a la izquierda?	ah lah eeth-kee-**er**-dah?
above/below?	arriba/abajo?	ah-**ree**-bah/ah-**bah**-hoh?

- **Asking a taxi driver to return for you**

English	*Spanish*	*pronounced as*
Please	Por favor	**Poor** fah-**voor**
take us to ...	llévanos a ...	Y**ay**-vah-nos ah ...

and return	y volver	ee vol-**vair**
for us at …	para nosotros a …	**pah**-rah nos-**oh**-tros ah …

Point out the time when you wish him to return on your watch.

An inexpensive phrase book will help you compose other 'key' phrases and answers.

Organisation of the walks

I hope that this book is set out so that you can plan your walks easily … depending on how far you want to go, your abilities and equipment, and what time you are willing to get up in the morning! You might begin by considering the fold-out touring maps inside the back cover. Here you can see at a glance the overall terrain, the road network, and the general orientation of the walking maps in the text.

Quickly flipping through the book, you'll find that there is at least one photograph for every walk. Having selected one or two potential excursions from the map and photographs, look over the planning information at the beginning of each walk description. Here you'll find distance/walking time, grade, equipment, and how to get there by public transport. If the walk appears to be beyond your fitness or ability, a short or alternative version may be given, which *does* appeal to you. On hot days, the picnic strolls described on pages 8-11 may be as strenuous an adventure as you'd like to tackle.

When you are on your walk, you will find that the text begins with an introduction to the overall landscape and then turns to a detailed description of the route itself. **Times** are given for reaching certain points in the walk. *Important: do* compare your own times with those in the book on one or two short walks, before you set off on a long hike. Remember that I've included only *minimal stops* at viewpoints; allow ample extra time for photography, picnicking, or swimming. Don't forget to take **transport** connections into account!

The large-scale **maps** (all 1:50,000; see page 34) have been set out facing the walking notes if the route is isolated, but where several routes converge, they are often presented on facing pages, to help with overall orientation. Below is a key to the symbols on the maps:

trunk road	spring, tank, etc	shrine or cross
secondary road	watercourse, pipe	church.cemetery
major track	P picnic suggestion (see pages 7-10)	stadium
other track	best views	danger! vertigo!
path, steps	bus stop.car parking	map continuation
3 → main walk	waypoint	*i* Visitors' Centre
3 → alternative walk	specific building	mill.cave
— 400 — altitude (m)	picnic site with tables	rock formation
		blow hole

WALKS

Photo: enormous colonies of ferns at Los Tilos

La Palma

Walk 1: FROM THE MIRADOR LA TOSCA TO GALLEGOS

Distance/time: 6.2km/3.8mi; 2h30min
Grade: ●❕ moderate-strenuous, with overall ascents of about 350m/1150ft. You must be sure-footed and have a head for heights. Not recommended in wet weather. *Red and white GR waymarking*
Equipment: walking boots, sunhat, sunglasses, suncream, raingear, long trousers, cardigan, windcheat, picnic, water
Transport: 🚐 from Santa Cruz (Línea 100) to the Barlovento terminus, then ongoing bus (Línea 120) to the Mirador La Tosca; journey time about 1h20min — or walk from Barlovento to the start of the walk (about 15min). Or 🚗: park in the space next to the *mirador* (28° 48.642'N, 17° 48.871'W). Return on 🚐 (Línea 120) from the Gallegos turn-off to the *mirador* to collect your car, or to Barlovento, then change to bus (Línea 100) back to Santa Cruz.

This is a roller-coaster walk. Crossing the isolated hills of the northeast, you dip into and out of *barrancos* all the way. But first, enjoy the stupendous view over the rugged north coast from the Mirador La Tosca (**P1**). It's a windswept landscape, where hamlets straggle down the dividing ridges; your hike will take you to Gallegos, the largest of these isolated outposts.

Start out at the **Mirador La Tosca** (⭕): walk back towards Barlovento along the main road (LP1). Take the first left turn (**7min**), along a concrete lane signposted 'GR130 — CAMINO REAL DE LA COSTA. GALLEGOS, SANTO DOMINGO'. Three minutes downhill, turn left on a path (signposted 'CAMINO REAL DE GALLEGOS'), descending into the *barranco*. You cross the floor of the *barranco*, passing fallow plots concealed amidst the heather. Soon you round a bend, to enjoy a magnificent view to the distant sea-cliffs on the north coast (**15min**). A path with steps joins you from the left.

Coming onto a driveway in **La Tosca** (❶), pass a house and bear left on the village lane. Ignore

Walk 1: From the Mirador La Tosca to Gallegos 43

minor turn-offs. After 200m, when you meet another lane on a bend (SIGNPOST), follow it to the right downhill. Two minutes later, this lane swings sharply right: go straight ahead on a concrete path (SIGNPOST), which soon reveals itself as the remains of the old cobbled *camino real*. If the *cumbre* is free of cloud, the white-domed observatory is visible.

Cross the floor of the **Barranco de Topaciegas** (❷), choked with vegetation. After a steep climb up the far side, ignore a path to the left. Keep straight on until you meet a concrete lane (**40min**; SIGNPOST) and follow it uphill to the left. Leave the lane after 30m/yds, turning right on a SIGNPOSTED PATH (❸). From here you have a good view of the *cumbre* with its seaward-tumbling ridges. Orchards and pockets of cultivation lie scattered across the landscape. Dropping down into another, deeper *barranco* (❹; **Barranco de la Vica**), your way is flanked by sticky *Cistus*. On reaching the other side of the *barranco*, the way is slightly vertiginous for a short stretch. Pass below an old goats' pen lying under a rock overhang.

Leaving the *barranco*, you come onto a road in **La Palmita** (❺; **1h**). Ascend the road, cross over another small road, and pick up the signposted continuation of your *camino* some metres uphill. It drops you down into another *barranco*, this one full of bramble bushes. On reaching a track, follow it to the right uphill. A minute later, at an intersection, keep straight on around the hillside. At the fork that follows, go right, downhill (SIGNPOST). Ignore minor tracks striking off left. Gallegos comes into view, looking deceptively close, but it's still two *barrancos* away.

Two minutes below the junction, the track veers right; take the path on the left (SIGNPOST), into the penultimate *barranco*, the **Barranco de Gallegos**. It's the most impressive ... and the most tiring! Winding down its vertical walls, you pass through a gate (please leave it as you find it). The path is at times vertiginous and, nearer the bottom, the way might be overgrown. Cross the STREAM BED on boulders (❻; **1h40min**). The climb out of this *barranco* is quite steep. Once out of the *barranco*, beyond another gate, you cross over a road which heads along the crest of the ridge (SIGNPOST). From here you have an excellent view of Gallegos, stepped down a declining rocky ridge. Now the path descends into the final ravine. Once in the bed of this *barranco*, pass some old cave dwellings and turn towards the sea to pick up your ongoing path out of the ravine.

Entering **Gallegos** (❼; **2h**), you reach the main lane at a junction. You could pick up the bus here for the return to your car or to Santa Cruz. Or you could visit the local bar, just 40m/yds downhill. Having quenched your thirst, and wanting to see more of this attractive little village, you have two options: Go straight up the road from the bar for 20 minutes, to the main road. The BUS STOP is just opposite the village exit (❽; **2h20min**).*

---

*There are plans to build a *mirador* above the coast in Gallegos (see the 📷 symbol on the map), with restaurant and skywalk; it is hoped that when it opens in 2021 it will bring more tourism to the north.

44 Landscapes of La Palma and El Hierro

Or, for a slightly longer route, turn right at the junction 40m up from the bar. Keep straight on through the simple PLAZA DE LA FUENTE. Picture-postcard dwellings with colourful gardens lie hidden in the midst of vegetable plots, vineyards, orchards and banana groves. Completing the village circuit, climb straight up the hillside for about 25 minutes, back to the main village lane. The main road and the BUS STOP are a minute further uphill (**2h30min**).

Overlooking the north of the island, with La Tosca in the foreground (Picnic 1)

Walk 2: LOS SAUCES • MIRADOR DE LAS BARANDAS • BARLOVENTO

See also photo on page 53
Distance: 12km/7.5mi; 4h10min
Grade: ●❗ strenuous, with an ascent of about 900m/3000ft overall. The path out of the Barranco de Herradura is steep, narrow and vertiginous. You must be surefooted and have a head for heights. Don't attempt in wet weather.
Mostly yellow/white PR waymarked
Equipment: walking boots, sunhat, sunglasses, suncream, fleece, raingear, picnic, plenty of water, walking pole(s)
Transport: 🚐 from Santa Cruz to Los Sauces (Línea 100); journey time 35min. Or 🚗: park in Los Sauces, either near the church, or one street to the west (28° 48.285'N, 17° 46.484'W). Return on 🚐 from Barlovento to Santa Cruz (Línea 100); journey time about 55min. Or the same line to Los Sauces, to collect your car.

The north boasts the most impressive ravines on the island, like the unmissable Barranco de Herradura. A forestry track leads you into this *barranco*, and a footpath not much wider than a pair of boots takes you back out of it. On the way in, you'll see magnificent colonies of La Palma's endemic blue *Echium* (viper's bugloss), a rival for Tenerife's *taginaste rojo* both in splendour and in height. *Woodwardia radicans*, a prehistoric fern with two-three metre-long stems, flourishes on the damp *barranco* walls.

Begin the walk at the BUS STOP in Los Sauces (**O**). Cross the street and walk 10-20m/yds to the left. Then go uphill (at the right of a park), past the Ayuntamiento (town hall) and the pharmacy. Keep straight uphill, climbing steeply. This village has an authentic farmyard feel about it. Some of the old homes will take you by surprise with their unusually bright colours, while the gardens display a mixture of flowers, fruit trees and vegetables.

A renovated AQUEDUCT on the left will catch your eye (**10min**). Just past the aqueduct, turn right (signpost: 'PICO DE LA CRUZ, MIRADOR TOPO DE LAS BARANDAS, PR LP7'). Not far uphill, the road forks. Both forks rejoin, but take the left fork — it's quicker. Once past the CAMPO DE FUTBOL, the climb steepens, as you rise through patchy cultivation. Soon after the forks have rejoined and the way has reverted to track, you reach the rim of **Barranco del Agua**, with an excellent view towards the *cumbre* from the **Mirador de Llano Clara** (**❶**; **30min**).

From this lookout point, leave the track and climb a cobbled path to the left (SIGNPOST). Several minutes up, on rejoining the track (SIGNPOST), follow it to the left uphill. The steadily ascending track winds through scrub, a mixture of laurels, heather, ferns, *codeso (Adenocarpus)*, and scatterings of old chestnut trees, while the Barranco de Herradura drops away to the right.

Ignore all turn-offs until you reach the turn-off left to the **Mirador de las Barandas** (**❷**; **1h10min**). From this *mirador* you enjoy the splendid view shown on page 53, looking straight down into the Barranco del Agua and across the heavily-wooded ridges that carve up the landscape.

45

The Laguna de Barlovento, with the eponymous village in the background

Return the 120m/yds to the main track, to continue the walk. Ignore a first track off right but, 10 minutes from the *mirador*, fork right on a clear track (**3**; signpost: 'LAGUNA DE BARLOVENTO, PR LP7.1'). Every now and then you'll see enormous viper's bugloss along the route. In summer their 2-3m/6-9ft-high stalks will be embellished with blue flowers. The native white-tailed and Bolle's laurel pigeons abound up here too. Ignore a faint track to the left after approximately 20 minutes (SIGNPOST). The prehistoric fern colonies *(Woodwardia Radicans)* along this part of the walk are the largest on the whole island.

Entering the **Barranco de Herradura**, the way becomes dark and shady. A rockfall has caused the track to narrow down to a path. As you approach the valley floor, notice the caves cut into the bank on the left, just before the track turns sharply to the right. A couple of minutes further along, go into the trees on a waymarked path. In just one minute you reach the **Galería Meleno** (**4**; **2h10min**), securely locked behind a metal gate. There's an ABANDONED BUILDING on the left side of the ravine; some endemic geraniums grow beside the track.

The continuing path begins at the right of the abandoned building and is steep and vertiginous at the outset. The slopes are sheer, but wooded, thus lessening the exposure ... at least psychologically. ***Important:*** *remember that the leaves covering the path are very slippery.* A good 10 minutes up, you round a bend and enter another shady mossy *barranco* with vertical walls; not only is this ravine so dark that it's difficult to appreciate its beauty, but your eyes *should* be glued to the path the whole time!

Close on 30 minutes up from the *barranco* floor, you rise to a

CREST (**5**; **2h40min**; PR LP7.1 SIGNPOST). The path takes you to a track, soon flanked by garden plots. The Laguna de Barlovento (a large reservoir) appears through the trees, with a *zona recreativa* to its right. The surrounding hills are being cleared of trees and scrub to create gardens and orchards. When you come to a T-junction, turn left (**6**; where a SIGNPOST points in the *opposite* direction). The *laguna* reappears not far ahead; later in the walk you will circle to the left of it.

Now ignore all side paths and tracks for the next 10 minutes, until you come to a MAJOR SIGN-POSTED JUNCTION (**7**): turn right here. Now keep to the main track, ignoring all side tracks. Twenty minutes from the major junction, weave your way past a few abandoned buildings (visitors' centres and museums for a 'rural interpretation park' which never got off the ground). Reaching a junction with a large orange building on the corner below, turn right and after a minute join the road to the **Laguna de Barlovento** *zona recreativa* (**8**; **3h35min**). Turn left; then, some 50m/yds along, leave the road: turn right on a track, heading into a cultivated basin. Ignore the fork to the right at the outset. Follow the same path/track, ignoring all turn-offs, until you reach the main road. Turn right for 150m/yds, then go left into a small industrial area.

When you reach the main road again, cross it and follow the track opposite, again ignoring side paths. Cross the road again and continue on a path, straight past cultivated fields and a housing estate on the left. Reaching the main Barlovento/Gallegos road, follow it to the left, then take the second right turn, just before a *casa forestal* (forestry house).

This brings you to the centre of **Barlovento**. The BUS STOP (**9**; **4h10min**) is 100m/yds below the Consultorio de Barlovento (health centre).

Walk 3: LAS LOMADAS • BARRANCO DEL AGUA • LOS TILOS • LOS SAUCES

See also photos on pages 46, 53
Distance/time: 10.8km/6.7mi; 3h35min
Grade: ●❗ strenuous. There's a lot of scrambling over rocks and boulders in the bed of the *barranco*, and ascents of about 700m/2300ft overall. You must be sure-footed and have a head for heights. Don't attempt just after rain or in very windy weather: the paths are dangerous if wet, and there is the possibility of rockfall in the *barranco*. *Yellow and white PR waymarking beyond Los Tilos*
Equipment: hiking boots, sunhat, sunglasses, suncream, windcheat, raingear, picnic, water, *torch*
Transport: 🚐 from Santa Cruz to Las Lomadas (🚐 Línea 100); alight just before the bridge over the Barranco del Agua; journey time 35min. *You will not see the bridge from the bus in time to alight, so make it clear to the driver that you are walking to Los Tilos.* 🚗 park just before the bridge over the Barranco del Agua (28° 47.778'N, 17° 46.250'W). Or park at Los Tilos (28° 47.388'N, 17° 48.130'W). Return on the same bus from Los Sauces, or walk back to your car (add 15min) — or, if parked at Los Tilos, take a taxi from the square in Los Sauces back to your car.
Short walk: Los Tilos — Barranco del Agua — Los Tilos (1km/0.6mi; 30min return). ● You must be agile: a riverbed scramble *with a danger of rockfall* (wear stout shoes with a good grip). *Not suitable in wet or windy weather.* 🚗 to Los Tilos (28° 47.388'N, 17° 48.130'W). From the car park walk down the asphalt road a short way, to locate a WATERCOURSE with adjacent path — on your right, 100m/yds before the bridge. Pick up the main walk at ❶ and follow it to the first rock face, then return.

There's no *barranco* like this one in the whole archipelago. Its virtually perpendicular walls are smothered in vegetation, and from its boulder-strewn floor you look up at the sky through cascading ferns and trees. In summer, only one thing is missing from the Barranco del Agua ... water. Narrow *canales* divert this precious commodity higher up the valley, transporting it to nearby villages and farms, and to a power plant that generates 10 per cent of the island's electricity.

The bridge over the Barranco del Agua at Las Lomadas is one of the longest and highest arch bridges in Spain.

The walk begins in **Las Lomadas**, at the BUS STOP just south of the BRIDGE (❶) over the **Barranco del Agua**. Follow the road signposted to 'LOS TILOS' into the *barranco*, then take the left turn (**15min**) and ascend the road towards Los Tilos. In about **1h** you cross the Barranco del Agua for the third time: 100m/yds further on, on a bend in the road, look below the road on the left for a WATERCOURSE WITH AN ADJACENT PATH (❶). *(The Short walk joins here and turns right on the watercourse.)*

Follow this path for a minute, until you reach a TANK, then take steps down into the bed of the *barranco*. (Or take the alternative route and go through the short TUNNEL in the right-hand side of the *barranco* wall — the tunnel is always lighted, but take your torch anyway, to be on the safe side.) Depending on the time of the year when you're walking and how much water is in the *barranco*, you should be able to venture from 10 minutes to half an hour upstream — scrambling over tree trunks, rocks and, eventually, boulders, and encountering steep drops. Sometimes a large WATERFALL (❷) about 200m past the tunnel will block your way — unless you want to get soaking wet! It's not always there, but in winter it acts as an overflow for some of the excess water in the *canals* above. **Only go as far as you feel comfortable and safe.** If you get far enough, you'll reach the end of the walkable part of the *barranco* — a sheer cliff face, where you will have to turn back.

Back on the road, turn left to the car park and restaurant at **Los Tilos** and, above these, the INTERPRETATION CENTRE (❸; 'Biosphere Reserve'; **2h**). There's a large picnic area below the centre but,

49

50   Landscapes of La Palma and El Hierro

for a more peaceful spot, try the setting shown below (Picnic 3): locate the watercourse two minutes' walk below the centre and follow it to the left for a few minutes. The path is vertiginous, but a handrail *(don't lean on it)* provides psychological support.

The next part of the walk is the tiring climb to the Mirador de las Barandas. Take the yellow/white waymarked path behind the centre (large board: 'CAMINO AL MIRADOR DE LAS BARANDAS'). After forking

Walk 3: Las Lomadas • Los Tilos • Los Sauces 51

left off the more prominent path about 10m/yds past the sign, there are no further turn-offs. Handrails along the vertiginous stretches help allay any fears, but *don't lean on them!* Thirty-five minutes up, and blue in the face, you reach the

Mirador de las Barandas (❹; **2h35min**; photograph page 53), with a shelter, tables and benches, and a water tap. From here you look straight up the ravine as it twists and winds its way into the laurel woods of the central massif. Los Tilos lies below, in the narrow V of the *barranco*.

To make for Los Sauces, follow the track from the *mirador* to the main track and descend right on the PR LP 7, ignoring all turn-offs. Through the trees and scrub you catch glimpses of the Barranco de Herradura (Walk 2), which soon drops away to your left. Some 30 minutes from the *mirador*, turn right on a cobbled path (SIGN-POST), just above an S-bend. After this short-cut you rejoin the main track on the very edge of the Barranco del Agua — with a bird's-eye view of the tremendous *barranco* of Los Tilos from the **Mirador de Llano Clara** (❺; **3h10min**).

Two minutes later the way becomes concreted and divides. Take the right fork, to begin the steep descent to Los Sauces. This pretty farming settlement is spread across a shoulder in the hillside, completely enveloped by banana plantations. Passing the *campo de fútbol*, you rejoin the left fork and continue downhill. A road joins from the right; a couple of minutes later, bear right at a fork. Multi-coloured houses briefly flank the street leading into the centre of **Los Sauces**. The BUS STOP (❻; **3h35min**) is to the left of the main square, opposite the CHURCH.

Left: watercourse at Los Tilos (Picnic 3); above: In the Barranco del Agua the walls, dripping with vegetation, tower overhead and block out the sun.

Walk 4: TWO VIEWPOINTS FROM LOS TILOS

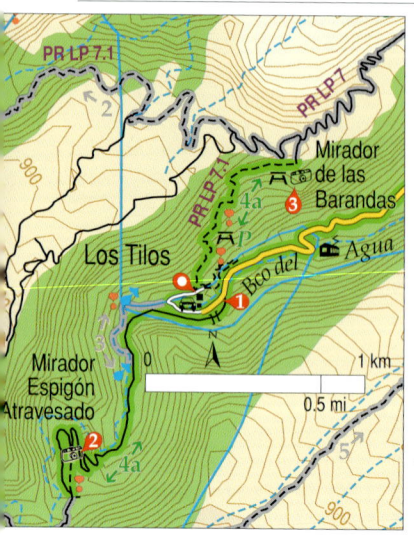

See also photos pages 40-41, 49-51
Distance/time: see Walks a and b
Grade: ● ❢ easy-moderate, but with a possibility of vertigo
Equipment: walking boots or stout shoes, raingear, jacket, trousers, picnic, water, *torch*
Transport: 🚌 to Los Tilos: either park at the Interpretation Centre (28° 47.388'N, 17° 48.130'W) or, if you are just doing Walk a, park at the foot of the first track on the left, 500m short of the Interpretation Centre (28° 47.487'N, 17° 47.977'W). Or 🚌 from Santa Cruz to/from Las Lomadas (Línea 100); alight just before the bridge over the Barranco del Agua; journey time 35min. (Allow an extra 55min *each way* from the bus stop by the bridge to the track where the walk begins and back down to the main road.)
Walk a: Mirador Espigón Atravesado (6km/3.7mi; 1h50min *from the visitors' centre;* 5km/3mi; 1h30min from the lower car park). Track walk for the most part, with an ascent/descent of 320m/1050ft overall; the final path to the viewpoint is vertiginous but protected.
Walk b: Mirador de las Barandas (2.4km/1.5mi; 1h). Ascent/descent of about 250m/820ft overall, on a *steep,* somewhat vertiginous path. Take care on the return: the descent is slippery!

Both of these short walks are ideal leg-stretchers during a car tour. Each focuses on the magnificent Barranco del Agua at the heart of the biosphere reserve — Walk a overlooks it from the south, Walk b from the north.

Start Walk a from the INTERPRETATION CENTRE (**○**): follow the road back the way you arrived for some 500m/yds, until you come to the lower Los Tilos parking area. Here take the track signposted 'MONTE EL CANAL Y LOS TILOS' (**❶**) that leads into the forest, the yellow/white waymarked PR LP 6. (Of course, if you are not doing Walk b, you could park here if there's room and start the walk here.) In about five minutes you go through a 100m/yd-long TUNNEL, emerging in a primeval *laurisilva* where the sun hardly penetrates. Just below to the right you can hear the tinkle of water in the canal followed in Short walk 3.

Beyond a STONE BUILDING (**30-40min**), the track climbs a bit more steeply. Eventually you come to a WIDE JUNCTION with an information board (**50min-1h**), from where Walk 5 continues ahead. Just below it, take the path and steps sharp left along a very narrow ledge (there are protective railings). This excitement lasts for about five minutes, until you come to the precarious and vertiginous — but brilliant! — **Mirador**

Walk 4: Two viewpoints from Los Tilos 53

Espigón Atravesado, a tiny fenced-in viewpoint looking out north over the ravine (❷; **1h-1h20min**). Return the same way to the Interpretation Centre — or first follow the track to where it ends at an old goods hoist, to take in even more of this green jungle.

Start Walk b behind the INTER-PRETATION CENTRE (◉): climb the steep yellow/white waymarked path (PR LP 7.1) ascending the hillside from the car park to the **Mirador de las Barandas** (❸; **35min**), shown below and described on page 55.

View straight down into the Barranco del Agua from the Mirador de las Barandas

Walk 5: CASA DEL MONTE • NACIENTES DE MARCOS • NACIENTES DE CORDERO • LOS TILOS

See also photos pages 40-41, 49-62
Distance/time: 12.2km/7.6mi; 4h15min
Grade: ●! very strenuous, with an ascent of about 150m/500ft and drawn-out descent of over 1000m/3300ft. You must be sure-footed and have a head for heights: for about 1h20min the walk follows a *canal* cut into the sheer *barranco* wall. Only attempt this walk during a spell of fine, stable weather, and turn back *immediately* if the weather deteriorates. ***Do not attempt the walk just after bad weather: there is a danger of rockfall and landslides*** (the walk may be closed due to rockfall). There are also 13 tunnels, some narrow: not recommended for those who suffer from claustrophobia! *Yellow/white PR waymarks on most of the route, as well as white/green poles from the Casa del Monte up to the springs of Cordero.*
Equipment: walking boots, raingear, jacket, trousers, picnic, water, *plus torch, large plastic bag, and an extra pair of socks* (tunnel 12 is as wet as a power shower: cover yourself and your rucksack!)
Transport: 🚗 to Los Tilos: park at the foot of the first track on the left, 2km up the Los Tilos road (500m short of the visitors' centre; 28° 47.487'N, 17° 47.977'W). Or 🚌 from Santa Cruz to/from Las Lomadas (Línea 100); alight just before the bridge over the Barranco del Agua; journey time 35min. (Allow an extra 55min *each way* from the bus stop by the bridge to the track where the walk begins and back down to the main road.) From Los Tilos 🚙 4x4 taxi to the Casa del Monte to start the walk — an exhilarating drive of some 50min on a dirt track. Taxis are available every day: either call and make an appointment with Toño (629-213435), Luis (616-418847) or Pepe (649-945481) — they all speak a bit of English — or just show up at Los Tilos on the day: a taxi will be on duty. In general the drivers arrive at Los Tilos between 09.00-09.30 and try to fill their taxis, so there may be a short wait. Cost €15 per person at press date.

This walk can be summed up in three words: exhilarating, breathtaking (in more ways than one), and tiring. You start the walk high up in an isolated valley, following an irrigation *canal* with 13 tunnels — a marvel of workmanship. It's my favourite walk on the island, even though cliff-hanging watercourses give me the jitters. Your reward is water splashing down out of the hillsides once you reach the *nacientes* (springs) of Marcos and Cordero. This is followed by a scramble over rocks and boulders through an impressive *barranco*, which is not unlike the one in the Caldera de Taburiente, until you eventually reach a good but long, drawn-out descent path through a 'jungle' of laurel woods.

Begin the walk at the drop-off point near the **Casa del Monte** (○), at a height of 1330m/4360ft, where a gushing open *canal* meets the track. There are some large boards here, with information about the trail. Follow the *canal* to the left through the laurel forest.

Walk 5: Nacientes de Marcos y Cordero to Los Tilos 55

You will be walking along this watercourse for about an hour and 20 minutes — sometimes you will need to scramble up onto the edge of it but, in general, the path runs alongside it.

After five minutes the views open up and an immense *barranco* lies at your feet, with drops of several hundred meters. A rickety railing offers some psychological protection, but *don't lean on it!* There are also many steep and narrow sections still without

Sometimes you'll be walking on the very lip of the canal, but usually there is an adjacent path.

56 Landscapes of La Palma and El Hierro

railings, so *please watch where you're walking **all the time***. *To appreciate the magnificent scenery, stop walking, then look!*

Some 10 minutes along the FIRST OF THE 13 TUNNELS presents itself; at the outset it seems straightforward — wide and high — but, just 10m/yds in, this changes drastically into a narrow passage with steps leading down into the dark. The floor is probably covered in puddles, so if you haven't worn waterproof walking boots, it's too late now! The THIRD AND LONGEST TUNNEL (❶; 350m/yds) is a narrow affair and quite a squeeze, very romantic … especially when you meet a group of 20 other sweaty hikers halfway through!

Continue winding your way around the steep hillside, taking in the tremendous drops and the game of clouds filling in the canyon from time to time.

After tackling the NINTH TUNNEL (**55min**) you get a grand view of what is still in store for you. To the right, strain to see your ongoing path to the springs of Cordero through a gap in the inaccessible-looking cliff face. Straight ahead is a dark vertical wall pierced with holes, where you'll encounter the (in)famous 12TH TUNNEL, where you'll have your 'power shower'. All the while, the sound of water gets stronger. Put all your cameras and other delicate equipment away and cover yourself up with plastic bags to tackle this 'amusement park tunnel', with water coming out of

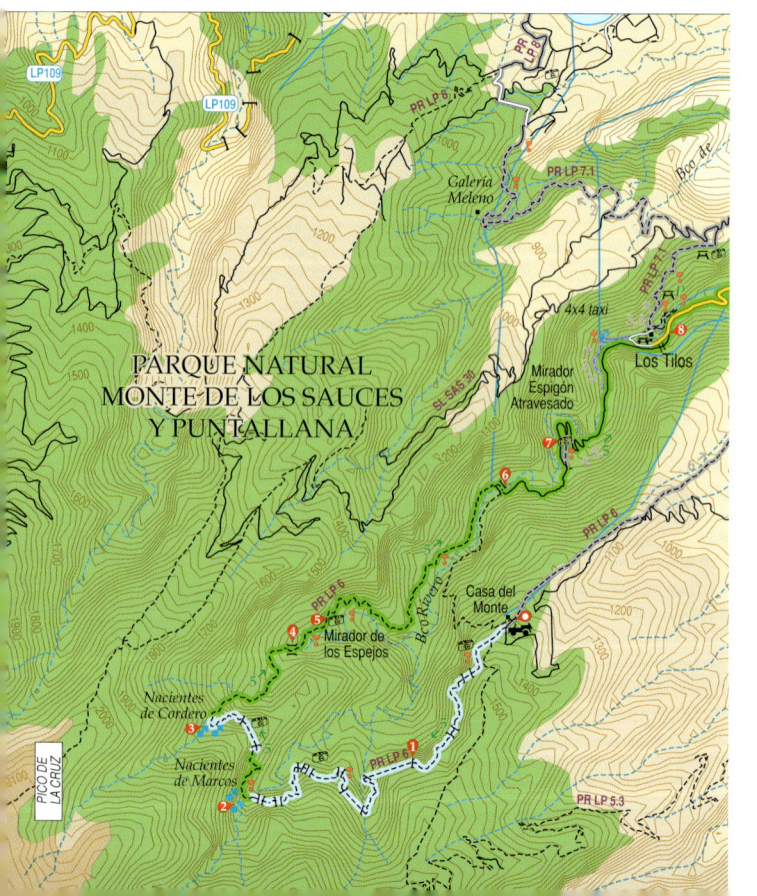

Walk 5: Nacientes de Marcos y Cordero to Los Tilos 57

the walls from all angles and a small river at your feet.

When you emerge in the sunshine at the other end, probably drenched, you reach the first springs en route, the **Nacientes de Marcos** (❷; **1h10min**), where water spouts out of the mountainside in small cascades.

Now haul yourself up the steep path up along the raging stream until you reach a higher *canal*. One more TUNNEL awaits you before you reach the second springs, the **Nacientes de Cordero** (❸; **1h30min**).

Leave the springs and head into the canyon by taking the clear path to the right of the springs. After five minutes you enter the riverbed and cross it. Some enormous boulders may appear to block your way, but waymarking guides you round them. Then follow the path on the left-hand side of the *barranco*, only to cross back to the other side after a few minutes. Stay on this path for 10 minutes and cross again to the LEFT SIDE OF THE RIVERBED (**1h50min**). When you regain the barranco bed after a good five minutes, follow it down to the left, scrambling (occasionally on all fours) over rocks, boulders and tree trunks, avoiding small puddles and wet walls dripping with beautiful colonies of prehistoric ferns, the *Woodwardia radicans*. Little light penetrates this dark fissure.

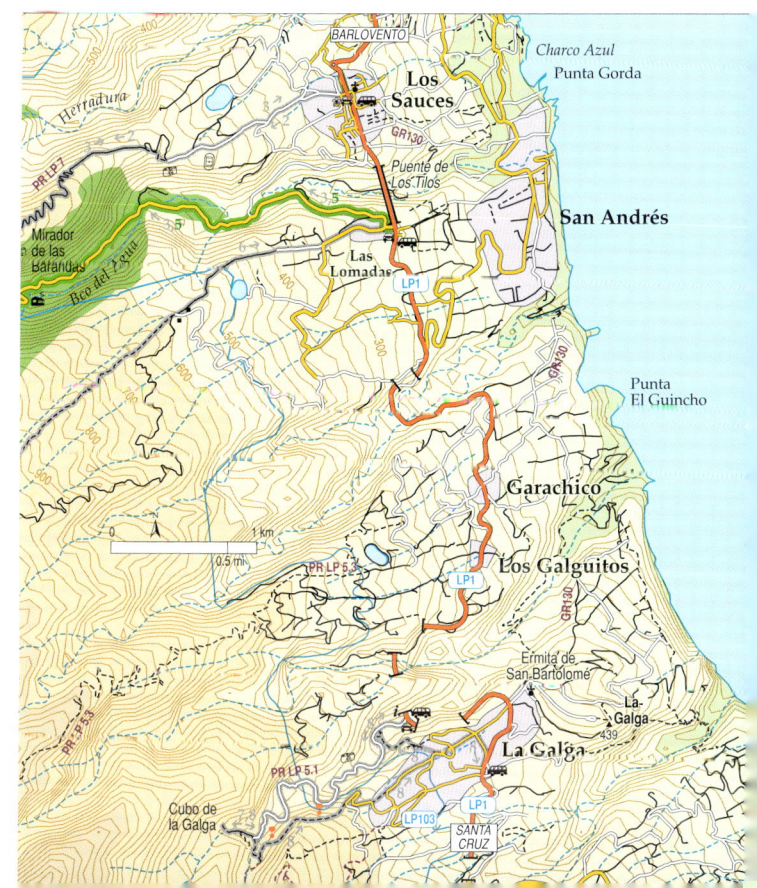

After 20 minutes in the *barranco* bed, you come to a SIGNPOST and a path on the right, which takes you across a WOODEN BRIDGE (④; **2h25min**). The torture is over, and you are now on a good but drawn-out path that will take you all the way down to Los Tilos. *But don't let your guard down:* in some places the path narrows, with steep drops. Eventually the valley opens up ahead and you come to the **Mirador de los Espejos** (⑤), where more fencing protects you as you peer down into the *barranco*.

But then you enter the laurel forest once more and, the further down you go, the more the path is shaded with dense foliage. After an hour down this path you cross the deep **Barranco Rivero** on another WOODEN BRIDGE (⑥; **3h25min**), this one more imposing (but *don't lean on the handrail!*). Climb up to the main Los Tilos track and follow it down to the left, again passing enormous colonies of ferns.

Ten minutes later, at a junction of paths and an INFORMATION BOARD, turn right up a narrow and vertiginous path to the **Mirador Espigón Atravesado** (⑦; **3h40min**), a brilliant view point overlooking the dense jungle of Los Tilos. *(Walk 4a comes up to this point from Los Tilos, then returns the same way)*. Then, ignoring all side paths, follow the main track down to the PARKING AREA below **Los Tilos** (⑧; **4h15min**).

Walk 6: CASA DEL MONTE • NACIENTES DE CORDERO • CASA DEL MONTE • LAS LOMADAS

See also photos pages 40-41, 49-55
Distance/time: 18km/11mi; 6h
Grade: ●! very strenuous, with an ascent of about 250m/500ft and drawn-out descent of over 1250m/4100ft. You must be sure-footed and have a head for heights: for a good 2h30min the walk follows a *canal* cut into the sheer *barranco* wall. Only attempt during fine, stable weather; turn back *immediately* if the weather deteriorates. Do *not* attempt the walk just after bad weather, as there is a danger of rockfall and landslides. There are 13 tunnels on this walk, some narrow: not recommended for those who suffer from claustrophobia! *Yellow/white PR waymarks on most of the route, as well as white/green poles from the Casa del Monte up to the springs of Cordero.*
Equipment: walking boots, raingear, jacket, trousers, picnic, water, *plus torch, large plastic bag, and an extra pair of socks* (tunnel 12 is as wet as a power shower: cover yourself and your rucksack!)
Transport: 🚐 from Santa Cruz to/from Las Lomadas (Línea 100; journey time 35min); alight just before the bridge over the Barranco del Agua. Then walk up to Los Tilos at the start of the day, when you are fresh (3km, with a height gain of 250m/820ft; 55min) — or try to hitch a ride up! From Los Tilos 🚙 4x4 taxi to the Casa del Monte to start the walk. See details on page 58. 🚗 Travelling by car, it's best to drive to Los Tilos, make taxi arrangements, then drive back to Las Lomadas to park and hop on the taxi to Casa del Monte.

This version of the hike to the Marcos and Cordero springs gives you the thrill of the *canal* stretch and the tunnels (twice!), but avoids the bouldery sections in the Barranco Rivero. The final stretch to Las Lomadas is via a beautiful tunnel-like path (to stay with the theme of the day) through the laurel forest.

Wilderness hike to the springs, with a bridge across the Barranco Rivero seen in the background

Begin the walk at the drop-off point near the **Casa del Monte** (**O**), at a height of 1330m/4360ft, where a gushing open *canal* meets the track. There are some large boards here, with information about the trail. Follow the *canal* to the left through the laurel forest. You will be walking along this watercourse for about two and a half hours — sometimes you will need to scramble up onto the edge of it but, in general, the path runs alongside it.

After five minutes the views open up and an immense *barranco* lies at your feet, with drops of several hundred meters. A rickety railing offers some psychological protection, but *don't lean on it!* There are also many steep and narrow sections still without railings, so *please watch where you're walking* ***all the time***.

Some 10 minutes along the FIRST OF THE 13 TUNNELS presents itself; at the outset it seems straightforward — wide and high — but, just 10m/yds in, this changes drastically into a narrow passage with steps leading down into the dark. The floor is probably covered in puddles, so if you haven't worn waterproof walking boots, it's too late now! The THIRD AND LONGEST TUNNEL (**1**; 350m/yds) is narrow and quite a squeeze, very romantic ... especially when you meet a group of 20 other sweaty hikers halfway through!

Continue winding your way around the steep hillside, taking in the tremendous drops and the game of clouds filling in the

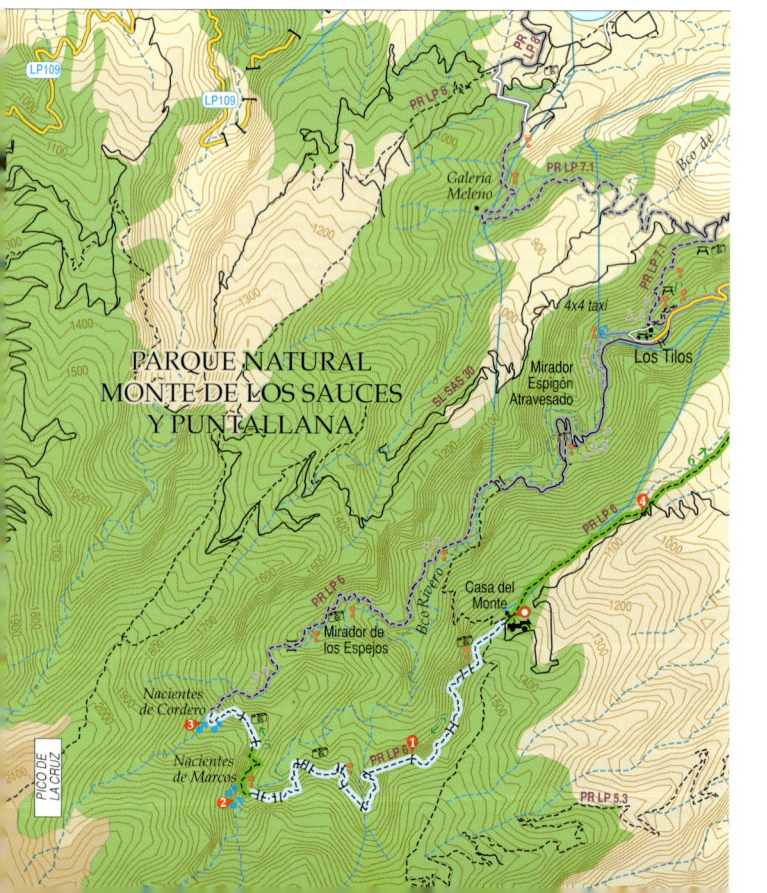

Walk 6: Nacientes de Marcos y Cordero to Las Lomadas

canyon from time to time.

After tackling the NINTH TUNNEL (**55min**) you get a grand view of what is still in store for you. To the right, strain to see your ongoing path to the springs of Cordero through a gap in the inaccessible-looking cliff face. Straight ahead is a dark vertical wall pierced with holes, where you'll encounter the (in)famous 12TH TUNNEL, where you'll have your 'power shower'. All the while, the sound of water gets stronger. Put all your cameras and other delicate equipment away and cover yourself up with plastic bags to tackle this 'amusement park tunnel', with water coming out of the walls from all angles and a small river at your feet.

When you emerge in the sunshine at the other end, probably drenched, you reach the first springs en route, the **Nacientes de Marcos** (❷; **1h10min**), where water spouts out of the mountainside in small cascades. Now haul yourself up the steep path up along the raging stream until you reach a higher *canal*. One more TUNNEL awaits you before you reach the second springs, the **Nacientes de Cordero** (❸; **1h30min**).

From here make your way back through the tunnels to the point where the taxi dropped you off in the morning near the **Casa del Monte** (O; **3h**). Turn right on a path opposite this building. Three minutes down, the path narrows and veers sharply left downhill.

For the next 30 minutes your

On this version of the Marcos and Cordero hike, you can enjoy the tunnel 'power shower' twice!

route goes straight down this dark, heavily-wooded ridgetop path, until you reach the MOTORABLE TRACK TO LAS LOMADAS (**4**; **3h30min**; SIGNPOST). *Don't* join the motor track here, but continue on the path; 10m/yds further down you rejoin the track (SIGNPOST). Walk 10m/yds to the left and then branch off on the path again (SIGNPOST). When you next meet the track, follow it 50m/yds down to the left to rejoin the path (SIGNPOST).

Next you emerge on a minor farm track: go 10m/yds to the right here, to pick up the path again, a deep trench cut into the hillside. A T-junction follows: turn right along the track. After one minute another track joins from the right. One minute later, at a three-way junction, cross a track and descend a COBBLED PATH (**4h05min**; SIGNPOST).

After five minutes the path meets the end of an overgrown track; turn left here. After another five minutes follow a concrete lane descending ahead. Two minutes later turn right along a track and, after 10m/yds, pick up the old path again. For the next five minutes keep straight downhill on this narrow path, beside a WATER PIPE. Meet a track and follow it to the left. Cross another track and after 25m/yds, you can pick up the washed-out path, on the left.

When you rejoin the MAIN TRACK at a fork, go left (SIGNPOST). At the junction 30m/yds further on, fork left (**5**; signpost: 'LAS LOMADAS'). Pass a WHITE BUILDING and continue downhill on a concrete lane. Los Sauces sits on the slopes opposite. From here, just keep straight downhill, first on the concrete lane and then an asphalt road. Passing through **Las Lomadas**, you reach the LP1. The BUS STOP is just where you join the main road (**6**; **5h** — or **6h**, if you walked up to Los Tilos to the taxi.

Walk 7: BARRANCO DE LA GALGA

See also photo pages 64-65
Distance/time: 6km/3.7mi; 1h35min
Grade: ● easy, with a gradual ascent of under 300m/980ft, all along a wide track. Recommended for everyone. *Yellow and white PR waymarking for much of the way; also green and white auto-guiding trail markings*

Equipment: walking shoes, raingear, cardigan, picnic, water
Transport: 🚌 from Santa Cruz to the north (Línea 100); alight at the second tunnel just after La Galga (bus drivers know the stop); journey time about 30min; same bus to return. Or by 🚗: park just before the second tunnel north of La Galga (28° 46.018'N, 17° 46.191'W).

This walk is ideal for 'first timers'. It's just straight up and straight back without any paths turning off to confuse you, and you get a taste of La Palma's ancient laurel forests without having to venture too far.

Begin at the BUS STOP AT THE TUNNEL (**O**): take the narrow road leading up the **Barranco de la Galga**, at the left of the INFORMATION HUT. Ignore the track descending to the left some 250m/yds along. From the outset you can see that this is a deep ravine, with walls matted in ferns and creepers. Billowing bushes of blackberry border the route. You pass a small grove of chestnut trees almost lost in this turmoil of vegetation. The sound of water trickling down the walls provides company for most of the way.

After **15min** the tarmac ends; the track passes below an AQUEDUCT (**❶**; **25min**) and soon the floor of the *barranco* fills with laurel trees. Fifteen minutes later both the *barranco* and the track FORK (**❷**; **40min**). First try the right fork. Ignore a turning left — to a water gallery — at a TURNSTILE (**❸**). The track ends in a clearing where a small trail with dense vegetation leads you further into a ROCK CAULDRON (**❹**). Quarrying once took place here, but now the massive escarpment has reverted to nature. After heavy rain a pretty

Laurel forest in the Barranco de la Galga

waterfall flows down the hanging valley opposite.

Return to the junction and turn right. This track ends after just 150m/yds, but a path leads up left to a small waterfall (in winter) in a few minutes. *Geranium canariense* abounds along the floor of the *barranco*. On the left lies a beautiful recess in the valley wall, the **Cubo de la Galga** (❺; **55min**), shaded by tall thin trees, where you will see a *canal* and a large water pipe. *(Walk 8 turns left just past the* canal.*)*

From here allow yourself about 40min to return to the BUS STOP ON THE MAIN ROAD (**1h35min**). If you've plenty of time to spare before the bus, there's a bar-restaurant in La Galga, 20 minutes uphill to the right, and another bus stop just beyond it (where a lane ascends to the right).

Walks 7 and 8: the Barranco de la Galga is one of the most beautiful corners of the Los Tilos biosphere reserve, where ancient laurels, ferns and creepers block out the sun.

Walk 8: CUBO DE LA GALGA CIRCUIT

See also photo page 63
Distance/time: 9.6km/6mi; 3h 10min (or 7.6km/4.7mi; 2h25min)
Grade: ●! moderate, with gradual ascents of 500m/1640ft overall; you must be sure-footed and have a head for heights for the return path which can be slippery and overgrown. *Yellow and white PR waymarking for most of the way*

Equipment: walking boots, rain-gear, cardigan, picnic, water
Transport: 🚐 from Santa Cruz to the north (Línea 100); alight at the second tunnel just after La Galga (bus drivers know the stop); journey time about 30min; same bus to return. Or by 🚗: park just before the second tunnel north of La Galga (28° 46.018'N, 17° 46.191'W).

This foray into the Barranco de la Galga is a more adventurous than Walk 7 and recommended for the sure of foot. From the Cubo de la Galga we rise to a terrific viewpoint over La Palma's northeast coast, then circle back down to the Cubo and retrace steps to the start of the walk.

Begin at the BUS STOP AT THE TUNNEL (○): follow WALK 7 all the way to the **Cubo de la Galga** (❺; **55min**). Facing the cliffs, take the path straight ahead that passes underneath the watercourse via a little arch. Then, at the junction, turn right on the PR LP 5.1 signed 'MIRADOR DE SOMADA ALTA'; the path on the left is a possible return trail later in the walk. The path rises steadily on log steps and crosses the **Barranco de la Galga** before meeting a TRACK (**6**). Turn left here, finally leaving the Barranco de la Galga. Continuing to rise (protective fencing shields some exposed stretches), after some 20 minutes you come to a wide dirt track and turn sharp left to the **Mirador de la Somada Alta** (**7**; **1h40min**), with a view straight down to the Cubo and along La Palma's northeast coast.

From the southeast edge of the *mirador*, now follow the PR LP 5 towards 'LA GALGA' — a sunken trail, accompanied by a water pipe. When the trail is interrupted by a dirt track, keep ahead in the same direction, edging the forest, until the sunken trail comes underfoot again. When you meet a crossing CONCRETE LANE (PR LP 5.1; **8**), turn left for 'CUBO DE LA GALGA'. Five minutes later, by a WATER-HOUSE (**9**), the main walk turns left for 'CUBO DE LA GALGA', climbing steadily, then dropping back down to the **Cubo** (**5**; **2h30min**), from where you retrace steps to the start (**3h10min**).

Or you can vary the return by turning *right* here (signpost: 'PR LP5.1, LA GALGA, SAN BARTO-LOME'. Walk downhill past a bus turning point, when asphalt comes underfoot. A few minutes later, on a big bend to the right, turn left downhill (same SIGNPOST) on a slippery cobbled path beside a pipe. Descending through a chestnut grove, continue on a concrete lane between fields and past a line of houses. Cross straight over a road, onto an embankment. A concrete lane follows.

If you came by car, turn left here (by a sign, 'PUNTO INFORMACION 1KM'; ●) and after 15m/yds turn right on a concrete path (a covered watercourse). After 50m/yds turn right on a narrow, overgrown trail and cross a water pipe. In 10 minutes you reach your outgoing lane. Turn right, back to the start.

If you came by bus, at the 'PUNTO' sign (●) cross the road again, keeping straight down on a concrete lane running under the road. Then cross the road once again and descend to the main road in La Galga. The BUS SHELTER (●; **2h25min**) is just to the right.

Walk 9: PUNTALLANA SPRINGS

See also photos on pages 8-9, 70
Distance/time: 5.6km/3.5mi; 1h45min
Grade: ●moderate, but with a steep climb of 200m/650ft at the end. Overall ascent/descent of about 250m/820ft. *Some green/white waymarking (SL PL 24); red/white GR waymarking at the end*
Equipment: stout shoes or walking boots, sun protection, cardigan, picnic, water
Transport: 🚌 from Santa Cruz to Puntallana (Línea 100); journey time 20min. Return on the same bus. Or by 🚗: park near the *ayuntamiento* (the town hall, 28° 44.376'N, 17° 44.701'W).

In years past, the springs around villages were of prime importance. Puntallana once counted 42 larger and smaller springs — some natural, a few with stone washbasins. It was not until 1978 that the whole village was connected to the municipal water supply. This walk takes you to some of the most important springs still in existence, but nowadays unused.

Start the walk in **Puntallana**, at the BUS STOP (**O**) opposite the TOWN HALL (*ayuntamiento*), with its large car park: walk north for just over 100m/yds, to the village CHURCH, San Juan Bautista. Then follow the road at the right of the church (Calle Processiones) downhill. You walk through the old part of the village, dotted with beautiful traditional houses. Going down the slope, your attention will be drawn to a large white traditional building above the houses, on the top of the hill opposite. This is the **Casa Luján**, which houses an ethnographic museum. In the barranco (valley) on your right you can already see the first spring, the Fuente de San Juan.

Casa Luján

Coming to a T-JUNCTION (**1**), turn right. Go down this street for 100m/yds, then turn right again. The house on your left here is the municipal *albergue* (hikers' hostel). The **Fuente de San Juan** (**2**) lies in a beautiful, tranquil setting under a canopy of plants and flowers. During the celebrations of the Fiesta de San Juan (24th June) the image of the saint is carried down to this spring in a procession.

Now return to **1** (the first T-junction) and go straight on. The road bends to the right; just 10m/yds further on, steps lead down to the next spring: **Fuentiña** (**3**), where you can see a series of washbasins not unlike those in the photo on page 73. This was the communal laundry in the old days.

Go back up the steps and turn right at the top. You pass some old farms and large fields, as well as some turnings to private properties and side tracks, all of which you ignore. Keep to this lane, now on concrete. It dips into a small valley with fruit trees. As you climb out again, leave the concrete lane just above a beautifully renovated house (signpost: 'FUENTE EL CORCHO, PLAYA DE NOGALES'). Just past the house this earthen track becomes an old footpath, lined with stones. It rounds another valley and climbs out just before a large yellow house (SIGNPOST; **35min**). Turn right here and go down the concrete lane for four minutes then, just past a green house, pick up the old footpath on the left (signpost: 'FUENTE IGLESIA'). This takes you into the next valley, where part of the trail may be slightly overgrown.

Just as you round the head of this valley, notice a small spring in the rock face in a tiny cave — **Fuente Flora** (**4**). Then an old cobbled path joins from the left: follow it down to the large **Fuente Iglesia** (**5**; **45min**), where there are more washbasins.

From Fuente Iglesia return seven minutes to the concrete lane with the signpost and turn left. Follow this lane downhill for some 15 minutes. It first edges a *barranco* on the left, then passes a large old cinder cone (**Montaña Loral**) and another impressive *barranco* on the right. You may notice some old cave dwellings in both *barrancos*.

Just above a hairpin bend in the road below you, where a large water pipe disappears into the ground, turn right on a partly cobbled footpath (**6**; signpost: GR130; **1h15min**). Walk past a picnic area and climb the path with wooden railings on the right. The path rounds the old volcanic cone in an easy but steep ascent. You pass some beautiful *pahoehoe* lava formations — and don't forget to look back; you can see as far north as Los Sauces and San Andrés.

Beyond some vineyards, you pass fields and houses and cross two tracks. A few minutes later meet the LP102 ROAD just past Cupalma, a large banana packing factory. Follow the road to the right for 30m/yds, then turn right on a signposted concrete lane, next to another banana shed (still the GR130). The old village of Puntallana with its beautiful traditional houses lies in front of you. Go left at a T-junction. A steep ascent follows. Pass the turn-off to the Fuente de San Juan and go left at the next junction. Climb steeply up to the new part of the village, the church and your BUS STOP/CAR PARK (**1h50min**).

Walk 10: PUNTALLANA, SHORT AND SASSY

See also photos pages 8-9, 67
Distance/time: 6.8km/4.2mi; 2h05min or 5.6km/3.5mi; 1h45min for motorists
Grade: ●easy-moderate, but with a steep climb at the end. Overall ascent/descent of about 240m/ 790ft. *Partly on green/white marked paths (SL PL 22, Fuente Benamas)*

Equipment: hiking boots, walking stick(s), sun protection, cardigan, water
Transport: 🚐 from Santa Cruz to/from Puntallana (Línea 100); journey time 20min. Or 🚗: park at the cemetery just above the roundabout at the Santa Cruz end of the village (28° 44.168'N,

This circuit above the village of Puntallana begins with a stiff-ish ascent on a beautiful woodland footpath and ends with a leisurely descent on a forest track. It leads you through agricultural areas, laurel and pine forest.

Start the walk at the **Puntallana** BUS STOP (●): walk back to the main road and cross at the large ROUNDABOUT, then walk up the road that leads to the CEMETERY (●) for 200m/yds. (Motorists start out here.) Take the tarred road to the left of the cemetery. Just at the

After about an hour's walking, the forest opens out to an area with bright red topsoil.

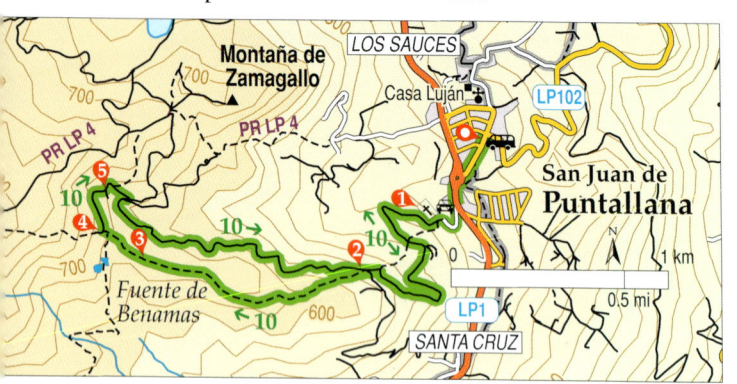

start, ignore a signposted steep path on the left. After a few minutes the tar ends and concrete comes underfoot for a short stretch. This quickly reverts to a red-soil track. Stay on this very clear main track for the next 15 minutes, ignoring all side tracks and paths. You very gradually climb up through different levels of vegetation, and the higher you climb the wider the views, until you come into the dense laurel forest.

Watch for another clear red-soil track heading sharply back to your left (❷; **35min**). Turn left here but, just 25m/yds further on, turn sharp right on a narrow trail. After a good 10 minutes of steep climbing on this trail, the path levels out in an area with dark red soil. A few shorter climbs follow. Occasionally a gap in the vegetation allows views towards the south as far as the airport and north towards Puntallana and the mountains.

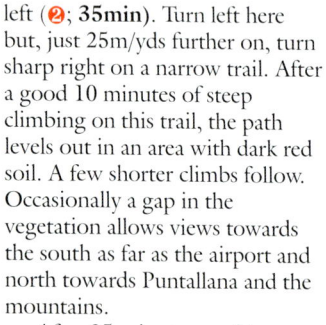

After 25 minutes on this beautiful, sometimes tunnel-like trail, the forest opens out to an AREA WITH BRIGHT RED VOLCANIC TOPSOIL (❸; **1h**). A few minutes later, you pass a trail on the left to the **Fuente de Benamas**, and just 7m/yds further on reach a crossing of paths and tracks (❹).

Go right here, down a track, ignoring minor side paths. After five minutes you reach the main track, where you turn right (❺; signpost: 'PISTA FUENTE BENAMAS'). Follow this main track downhill until, 25 minutes later, you come back to ❷, where you turned off earlier in the walk. Another 20 minutes takes you down to the CEMETERY (❶), to pick up your car — or continue down to the BUS STOP in the village

Puntallana's Iglesia San Juan

Walk 11: FROM TENAGUA THROUGH THE JUNGLE TO THE *LAVADEROS* IN THE BARRANCO DEL AGUA

See also photos on pages 8-9, 67 and 70
Distance/time: 5.2km/3.2mi; 1h30min as a circuit — or 6km/3.7mi; 2h to end in Puntallana
Grade: ● moderate, with an ascent/descent of 355m/1170ft for the circuit or an ascent of 355m and descent of 280m/920ft to end in Puntallana. *Partly red/white GR130, partly yellow/white PR LP 4.1*

Equipment: hiking boots, walking stick(s), long trousers, sun protection, cardigan, picnic, water
Transport: 🚌 (Línea 100) from Santa Cruz to/from the last bus stop in Tenagua ('la última parada en Tenagua'); journey time 15min. Or 🚗: park near the bus stop, on the main LP1, some 300m north of the petrol station (28° 43.217'N, 17° 44.775'W)

This walk to old water basins *(lavaderos)* hidden deep in the 'Valley of Water', offers two different endings: one returns to the starting point (for motorists); the other option continues to the village of Puntallana, from where you can return by bus or taxi. After seeing this 'laundry facility' deep in the jungle, you can understand why people washed their clothes and bed linen only once or twice a year!

Start the walk at the last bus stop in **Tenagua** (coming from Santa Cruz, **O**): cross the road to the yellow bus shelter and walk up the street called Calle La Lomadita. (signpost: 'GR130 SANTA CRUZ'). After 50m/yds turn left up a steep slope and keep left, still on Calle La Lomadita. At the top turn left again. Then, after 70m/yds turn right (signpost: 'PR LP 4.1') again up a steep concrete slope between houses. When the concrete stops at the entrance to a small white house, continue on an old cobbled footpath (signpost: 'PR LP 4.1 PICO DE LA NIEVE').

The old path follows several large WATER PIPES and climbs between fields and forest.

Eventually you reach a patch of red sandy soil where the water pipe disappears. Continue straight on. A few minutes later, on coming to a concrete road, follow it to the left. On your right is a large GOAT FARM with over 100 animals. After three minutes turn right off the road onto a footpath (❶; SIGNPOST). This leads below another (ugly) farm and after five minutes meets a signposted track, where you go left.

Just under 100m/yds after turning left on the track, step over the WATER PIPES on your right and take a path going down into the **Barranco de Agua** (❷; SIGNPOST; **35min**). The vegetation thickens, and all around you are tall laurel trees. After some seven minutes you pass below a HIGH STONE WALL on your left, part of an old water basin. Then, 20m/yds further on, the path forks (❸; SIGNPOST). Go left. (Later you will return to this point and take the other fork).

Following some old water pipes, after a few minutes you reach the bottom of the valley. Occasionally you will have to scramble over rocks and logs in this dry riverbed. Five minutes along this jungle-like valley, you reach the *lavaderos*, fed by a spring, the **Fuente del Tanquito** (❹; **50min**). Some of these basins were used for washing, some for bathing, some reserved for people with contagious diseases. A large information board gives an explanation in four languages.

Now return through the dry riverbed to the last junction at ❸ and go left downhill, towards a larger WATERWORKS and a *canal*. Ten metres further on, just below the first water deposit 'tower', turn right through brambles for 30m/yds and then climb up on a LOW STONE WALL. Follow the wall for about 65m/yds before climbing down again using the SHORT LADDER placed there to help you (❺; **1h**). Now just take this beautiful wide track out of the *barranco* until you meet the LP1 (❻; **1h20min**), where you have a choice.

If you want to return to your car from here, cross the LP1 and take the road on the outside of the tunnel. Follow it to the right (south). You will reach your car or the last BUS STOP in **Tenagua** in 10 minutes, for a total walking time of **1h30min**.

If you want to continue the walk to the village of Puntallana, turn left (north) and after 100m/yds, pick up the red/white-waymarked GR130 on the left. It climbs steeply for 10 minutes, to **Santa Lucia**. At the top, the first building you see is the **Casona de los Lugos**, a beautiful old mansion built around 1500, now in a state of disrepair. Just below it is the small CHAPEL of **Santa Lucia** (❼; also 16th century).

Walk up to the chapel, then down the concrete ramp and onto the road below (Calle El Calvario). Turn left here and follows this road for about 15 minutes, until it meets the LP1. Cross it and turn right for 100m/yds to pick up the GR130 again by turning sharp left below the road on a concrete track (❽; SIGNPOST). A few minutes later this changes to dirt track, then narrows to a footpath.

When you meet a concrete lane, follow it uphill, past some houses. Fifty metres/yards further on, at a T-junction, continue straight on (left). The lane again becomes a footpath. Cross a road above a very colourful housing estate and continue on a concrete lane lined with street lamps. Then cross the end of a road and continue on an old path, now passing a small *fuente* (spring).

The 'laundry facility' deep in the jungle-like surrounds of the Barranco del Agua. When you've hiked here, you may realise why people only washed their clothing and bed linen once or twice a year!

Reach another concrete lane and follow it to the left. A minute later you come into the village of **Puntallana** just below the school. The BUS STOP (**9**; **2h**) is 200m/yds to the right.

(PICO DE LA NIEVE TURN-OFF) • PICO DE LA CUMBRECITA • ERMITA DE LA VIRGEN — NATIONAL PARK VISITORS' CENTRE

Maps pages 84-85
Distance: 16.5km/10.2mi;

Grade: ●❗ moderate but long, with an initial ascent of 350m/1150ft and a descent of 1400m/4600ft. Accessible to all sturdy hill walkers who are sure-footed and have a head for heights, but only suitable in fine weather. Avoid on very windy days. At times the path may be overgrown with *codeso*. **Important:** *Weather conditions can change rapidly; be prepared! If cloud descends,* **utmost care** *is needed, as the walk edges the rim of the crater for much of the way. Both yellow/white (PR) and red/white (GR) waymarking*

Equipment: walking boots, sunhat (and something to tie it on with!), sunglasses, suncream, long-sleeved shirt, long trousers, fleece, warm jacket, gloves, raingear, picnic, plenty of water

Transport: 🚕 taxi to the Pico de la Nieve turn-off on the LP4; journey time 35min from Santa Cruz. Return on 🚌 from the National Park Visitors' Centre (Línea 300) — to Santa Cruz or Los Llanos.

Short walk: LP4 (Pico de la Nieve turn-off) to Pico de la Nieve and return (4.7km/3mi; 2h). ● Easy-moderate ascent of 350m/1150ft. Equipment and access as main walk or 🚕 *(4x4 only!)* to a parking area at the end of the track to Pico de la Nieve (28° 43.974'N, 17° 49.739'W) — saves 100m/330ft; 20min of climbing. Follow the main walk to the 1h15min-point at ❺, then turn left. Ten minutes later rejoin your outgoing path at ❷ and turn right downhill, back to your car.

Alternative walk 1: Circuit from the Ermita de la Virgen del Pino to the Refugio de la Punta de los Roques (17km/10.5mi; 6h10min). ●❗ Very strenuous, with an ascent of 1150m/3770ft. Only suitable in fine weather. Equipment as main walk. Access by 🚕: park at the *ermita*, north of the National Park Visitors' Centre (28° 39.773'N, 17° 50.506W). Or 🚌 to/from the National Park Visitors' Centre (Línea 300; journey time from Santa Cruz 25min; add 30min *each way*). Referring to the map opposite, follow the main walk in reverse to ❼; return the same way.

Alternative walk 2: see page 82.

I consider this one of the top walks in the Canaries. Circling the Caldera de Taburiente, often on its very rim, spectacular views unfold. On the descent the outlook sweeps across the plain of Los Llanos, over the volcanoes of El Pilar, and along the *cumbre*. If you're reasonably fit, this is *one walk you've got to do!* And the good news is that a taxi or hired car will do most of the climbing for you.

Start out at the PICO DE LA NIEVE TURN-OFF (⓿). Walk up the LP4 for 10m/yds, then take the hillside path above the road (signpost: 'PICO LA NIEVE, PR LP 3'). After a couple of minutes, the path swings back left, then climbs a gentle slope and widens out. Cairns mark the way through a typical Canary pine forest — spacious and with a floor clear of scrub. The path takes you to a CAR PARK (*where the Short walk can begin and end;* ❶; **20min**) and continues uphill for another

74

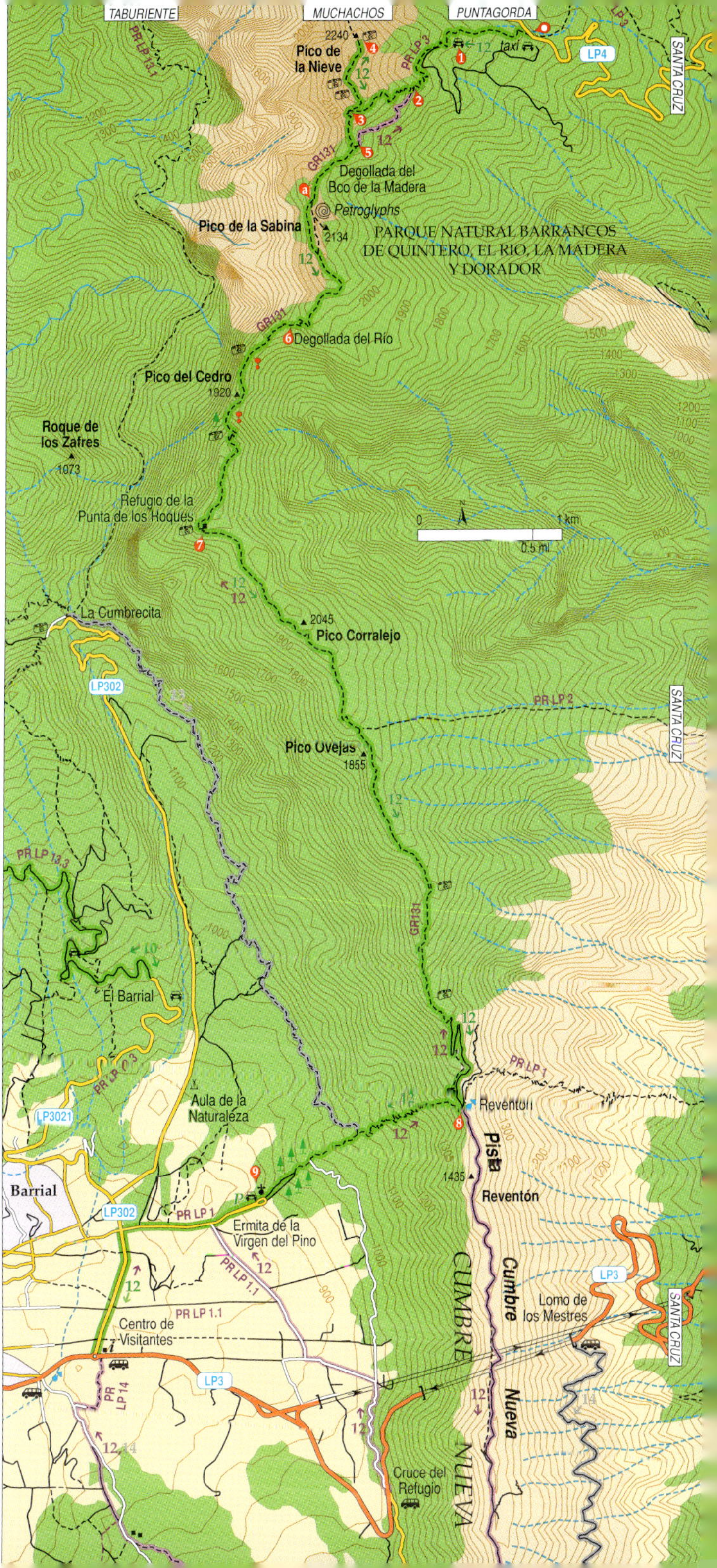

TABURIENTE
MUCHACHOS
PUNTAGORDA
SANTA CRUZ
LP4
Pico de la Nieve
2240
taxi
Degollada del Bco de la Madera
Petroglyphs
Pico de la Sabina
2134
PARQUE NATURAL BARRANCOS DE QUINTERO, EL RIO, LA MADERA Y DORADOR
GR131
Degollada del Río
Pico del Cedro
1920
Roque de los Zafres
1073
Refugio de la Punta de los Roques
0
1 km
0.5 mi
La Cumbrecita
2045
Pico Corralejo
LP302
PR LP 2
Pico Ovejas
1855
PR LP 13.3
El Barrial
PR LP 1
Aula de la Naturaleza
Reventón
LP3021
Barrial
PR LP 1
Pista Reventón
1435
Ermita de la Virgen del Pino
PR LP 1.1
LP3
Lomo de los Mestres
Cumbre Nueva
Centro de Visitantes
CUMBRE NUEVA
PR LP 14
Cruce del Refugio

Right: a noticeable weather-beaten cedro *is passed just before the refuge; right: view south from the Refugio de la Punta de los Roques over the El Paso basin to the Cumbre Vieja*

15 minutes; here you turn right on the path to the summit (**2**; SIGNPOST). Your view stretches across the forested shoulders of the *cumbre* — on clear days to Tenerife and La Gomera in the distance. Santa Cruz sits far below.

Approaching the edge of the crater, turn right uphill on the GR131 (**3**; signpost: 'ROQUE DE LOS MUCHACHOS'). (Ignore signposting for the Refugio del Pilar to the left.) At the next fork, keep left (the right-hand fork leads to Roque de los Muchachos). From the SUMMIT OF **Pico de la Nieve** (**4**; **1h**) a breathtaking view opens before you, of a deep cauldron lined by sheer ridges. The white buildings peeping over the crater walls on the right belong to the observatory shown on page 18.

Return to the first Roque de los Muchachos junction and turn right; turn right again at the next fork (**3**; signpost: REFUGIO DEL PILAR). Along this stretch, several short paths branch off right to viewpoints on the edge of the *caldera*. A PATH JOINS FROM THE LEFT (**5**; **1h15min**); follow it to the right. (*But for the Short walk, turn left.*) After a few minutes, you cross the pass of **Degollada del Barranco de la Madera**. Here you'll notice some very colourful rocky outcrops rising out of the crater wall.

A few minutes later you encounter a signposted turn-off left to some petroglyphs (●; signpost: 'PETROGLIFO TAGOROR PICO DE LA SABINA') and, above and to the right, a sign indicating some old corrals. Some 200m further on the petroglyph detour path rejoins, then you pass a bald gravel mound in hues of mauve, pink, smoky blue, and rusty brown.

The next section of the hike is the most striking. A zig-zag descent leads you down and across another pass—the **Degollada del Río** (**6**; **2h05min**). The ridge here is narrow and slides away on either side of the path. The huge valley to the left is the Barranco de la Hortelana, while to the right the crater just opens into a bottomless abyss. A steep climb follows, up the side of a precipitous jagged crag. Back on the inside of the crater, you pass by the eye-catching weather-beaten *cedro* shown above. Ahead is a magnificent viewpoint. In the depths of this cataclysm of rock, you can see the floor of the Barranco de Taburiente and a corner of the Playa de Taburiente U). Then you round a bend and arrive at the **Refugio de la Punta de los Roques** (**7**; **2h35min**). Although there is no heating, and fires are prohibited, the shelter may be welcome nonetheless. There are wooden bunks where you can lay out a sleeping bag, and

Walk 12: From Pico de la Nieve to the Visitors' Centre

water is available in bottles. The slope falling from the refuge overlooks the extensive open valleys of El Paso and Los Llanos.

The big hump of a mountain bordering the *caldera* on the south side is Bejenado (Walk 19), with Cumbre Vieja (Walk 17) in the background.

Continuing, pick up the path below the refuge. The route descends the *cumbre*, never straying far from the crest. Ignore a path to the left 10 minutes past **Pico Corralejo** (PR LP2) and another five minutes past the sign for **Pico Ovejas** (PR LP2.1). The western side of the *cumbre* opens up, affording another fine view over Santa Cruz.

The path finally drops down onto the **Pista Cumbre Nueva**. Continue ahead on this wide forestry track. Some 20 minutes later you arrive at **Reventón Pass** (❽; **4h25min**), where there is a WATER TAP (but outside winter and spring it may well be dry). Fork right downhill here on the PR LP 1 (signpost: 'ERMITA DE LA VIRGEN DEL PINO').

A beautiful old cobbled path leads you down the steep slope, below trees festooned with lichen and beside moss-covered rocks. A basin of small fields lies below. Five minutes down, a path joins from the right. Some 30 minutes down, you descend a splendid 'avenue' of regal Canary pines, some reputedly 400 to 500 years old. A signposted path from La Cumbrecita joins from the right here. Five minutes later you join a faint track leading to the **Ermita de la Virgen del Pino** (❾; **5h15min**; Picnic 12).

The National Park Visitors' Centre is just under half an hour away: follow the road from the chapel and, after 15 minutes, at a junction, turn left. On reaching the LP3, turn left again to the **Visitors' Centre** (**5h45min**). The Santa Cruz bus stops opposite.

Alternative walk 2: Cruce del Refugio — Ermita de la Virgen del Pino — Reventón Pass — Refugio El Pilar — National Park Visitors' Centre (16.5km/10mi; 5h20min).

● Strenuous, with an ascent of 620m/2035ft. Equipment as main walk. Access by 🚌 to Cruce del Refugio (Línea 300); journey time from Santa Cruz 25min.

From the junction where you leave the bus at **Cruce del Refugio** (〇), walk north along the main road for 50m/yds, then turn left on a country road. Referring to the map, follow roads to the **Ermita de la Virgen del Pino** (❶; 40min) and then ascend to the **Reventón Pass** (❷; 1h55min). There is a WATER TAP here, but outside winter and spring it may be dry.

Turn right at the pass on the **Pista Cumbre Nueva** and follow the red/white waymarked GR131

Right: striding along the cumbre *on the descent to the Reventón Pass during the main walk.
Below: leaving the Cruce del Refugio, you soon look across a basin of fields criss-crossed by stone walls.*

either along this track or the path beside it. You look straight across to Pico Birigoyo, setting for Walk 18. PR LP 18 comes in from the left just before the path rejoins the wide track, and you reach the LP301 road. Turning right, you soon come to the **Refugio El Pilar** (❸; 3h35min; Picnic 12b).

To end the walk, either use the map opposite or pick up Walk 14 at the refugio — waypoint ❹ *in Walk 14*. Highlights on the descent are the Llano del Jable and Montaña Quemada, before you come to the BUS STOP opposite the **National Park Visitors' Centre** (❹; 5h20min).

Aula de la Naturaleza
Reventón
Pista Reventón
Barrial
Ermita de la Virgen del Pino
Valencia
Centro de Visitantes
EL PASO, LOS LLANOS
SANTA CRUZ
Lomo de los Mestres
CUMBRE NUEVA
Cumbre Nueva
Cruce del Refugio
0
1 km
0.5 mi
Mña de Enrique
1261
Mna Quemada
1366
PARQUE NATURAL CUMBRE VIEJA
Llano del Jable
Pista Cumbre Nueva
SAN ISIDRO
La Pared Vieja
Refugio El Pilar
1505
1512

Walk 13: FROM LA CUMBRECITA TO THE ERMITA DE LA VIRGEN DEL PINO AND THE VISITORS' CENTRE

See also photos on pages 22 and 36
Distance/time: 8.5km/5.3mi; 3h15min
Grade: ●❗ moderate, with ascents of about 145m/475ft and descents of 615m/2020ft overall. You must be sure-footed and have a head for heights: part of the walk follows very narrow paths beside a steep cliff face, with steep drops below (see photo opposite). Some yellow/white waymarks (PR LP 1) near the end, but most of the *barrancos* and water galleries en route are signposted. *Not advisable in rainy or stormy weather.*
Equipment: sturdy walking shoes or boots, raingear, cardigan or fleece, water, walking poles
Transport: 🚌 (Línea 300) to the Visitors' Centre above el Paso; journey time 20min. Or by 🚗 (28° 39.209'N, 17° 51.165'W). Then taxi to La Cumbrecita (at time of writing €10-12).

This spectacular roller coaster hike heads south from the Cumbrecita viewpoint below impressive vertical cliffs. The first half of this walk is on a narrow path hugging the cliff (see opposite), the second half on wider paths and tracks through forest, passing old water galleries (see page 36) and agricultural areas. In the last half hour you follow a country road back to the Visitors' Centre.

Start the walk behind the wooden INFORMATION HUT (**○**) at the **Cumbrecita** VIEWPOINT. Walk down the slope for 60m/yds and turn right at the path junction (signpost: 'ERMITA PINO DE LA VIRGEN', INFO BOARD). The trail hugs an impressive vertical ROCK WALL at the outset, the result of an enormous gravitational collapse some 566,000 years ago which resulted in a rock avalanche and created the Los Llanos Valley.

After 10 minutes you pass the **Barranco Juan Flores**, with a dry waterfall and a wooden bridge. Continue through the pine forest of the indigenous species *Pinus Canariensis Sweet*, an almost completely fire proof pine! The path rises up to a VIEWPOINT (**❶**) with wooden railing from where you have a good view back to la Cumbrecita.

Cross the **Barranco de Guedea** and ten minutes later **Barranco del Salto de la Pantanera** (**35min**) Now the trail descends slightly and passes an old water station and some ancient concrete pipes in the **Barranco de Tabercorade**, where you come to the first *galería*, the **Galería de Tabercorade** (**❷**). The path climbs up to cross a valley of fallen pines and levels out again in the **Barranco de la Madera** (**1h**), only to climb again afterwards.

Cross the **Barranco de la Laja Azul** and shortly after, reach the eponymous VIEWPOINT (**❸**), from where you can see the meadows in the higher part of the El Paso valley. The path now descends steeply to the boulder-strewn bed of the canyon, where you continue the walk, ignoring a path to the right. Shortly after, you reach another *galería*, the **Galería de la Laja Azul** (**❹**), where the path widens and continues towards the right.

A few minutes further down, at a cross on the wall, ignore a faint track to the right and pass the **Lavaderos Fuente del Pino** (**❺**,

In the second part of the walk you ascend a narrow trail beside this rock wall.

1h25min), where in years past the women of the area came to do their washing in the spring water.

A few minutes later meet yet another water 'mine', the **Galería Intermedia** (**6**); here, at a crossing of tracks and trails, go left on the signposted path. A short climb follows beside enormous composite boulders (volcanic agglomerates), then the path comes out of the trees and passes an almond orchard.

Cross the **Barranco Juan Caitano** (1h45min) and a minute later reach the Galería Única (**7**). Turn right and almost immediately left to continue (SIGNPOST). Just

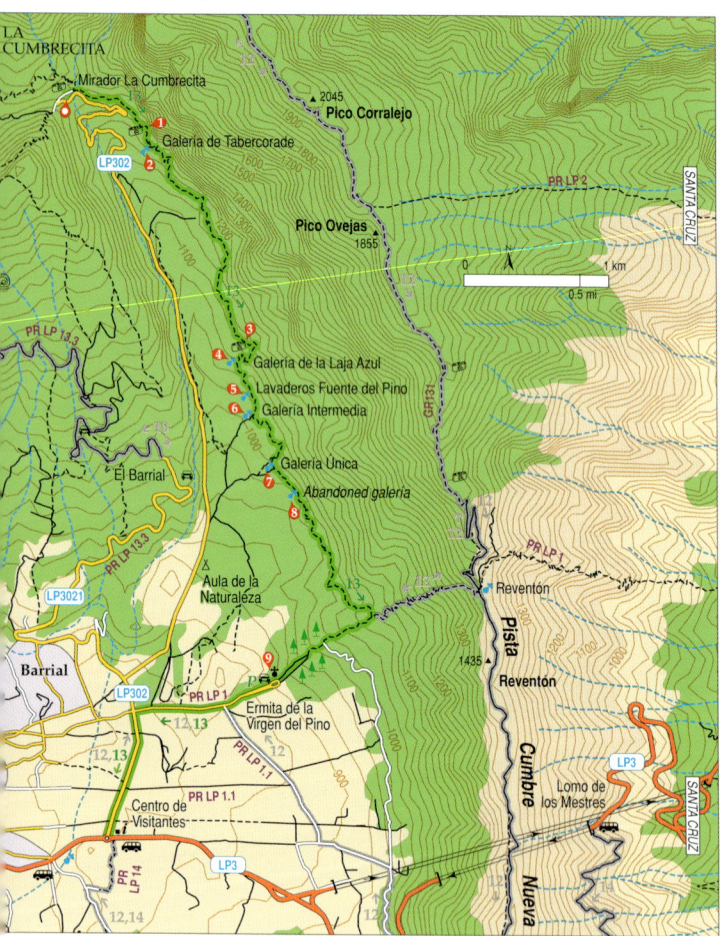

100m/yds further on, turn left again (SIGNPOST) and pass more orchards, some gigantic rock formations — and an abandoned *galería* (**8**): the miners quickly reached the basal complex and gas-holding layers, and realising they had no chance of finding water, the mine was closed off and gated.

Ten minutes later you descend through an area of burnt pines. On reaching **Lomo Padrón**, turn uphill beside a fenced-in property with dogs providing background music. There follows your last ascent: to the CREST above the *ermita*, where you join Walk 12 descending from Pico de la Nieve and turn downhill through a CENTURIES-OLD PINE FOREST.

In 15 minutes you reach the **Ermita de la Virgen del Pino** (**9**; **2h45min**), graced by a pine that may be 500 years old. Continue down the road: in 15 minutes turn left at the Cumbrecita junction. In another 15 minutes or less you'll be back at the **Visitors' Centre** (**3h15min**), to retrieve your car or take the bus from the stop opposite.

Walk 14: LOMO DE LOS MESTRES • LA PAI[...] REFUGIO EL PILAR • NATIONAL PARK VISITO[...]

See also photo on page 87
Distance/time: 14km/8.7mi; 4h10min
Grade: ● easy-moderate, with a gradual ascent of 450m/1500ft and a descent of 620m/2035ft. Not recommended in wet weather. *Yellow/white PR waymarking most of the way. Note: new paths and tracks are laid out in this area every few months, for wood-cutting and to reach newly-established fields. Some new paths and tracks may be missing from the text and the maps, but the walk is easily followed if you watch for the signposts and waymarks. Around the Pared Vieja picnic area, do not follow the small white/green signposts, but the white/yellow waymarking.*
Equipment: walking shoes (or boots), sunhat, sunglasses, suncream, raingear, fleece, windcheat, picnic, water
Transport: 🚐 Los Llanos bus *from Santa Cruz* (Línea 300); journey time 20min. *Important:* There are two tunnels on the LP3 below the Cumbre Nueva, and traffic is one-way: from Santa Cruz to Los Llanos through the old tunnel and from Los Llanos to Santa Cruz through the newer, lower tunnel. **This walk is only accessible from the older tunnel.** If you are taking a bus from Los Llanos, you must go into Santa Cruz and then switch to a bus travelling *back* to Los Llanos. (If you are travelling by taxi from Los Llanos, your driver will have to go through the new tunnel first, then head back up the *cumbre* towards the old tunnel.) Before you board a bus, ask the driver for **'la entrada del túnel viejo de la cumbre, la pista que va a la Pared Vieja'**; if necessary, show the driver this text or the map. Do *not* board unless you have the driv[...] because you cann[...] tunnel and walk b[...] cycling through th[...] forbidden. (In the past, some bus drivers were refusing to stop outside the tunnel, but now it has been made an official stop — although the sign is still missing — so there should be no problem.) Return on 🚐 the same bus from the National Park Visitors' Centre; journey time 40min to Santa Cruz.

Short walk: Refugio El Pilar — National Park Visitors' Centre (6.5km/4mi; 2h). Easy, with a descent of 620m/2035ft. Equipment as main walk. Access by 🚕 taxi or with friends to the Refugio El Pilar (28° 36.845'N, 17° 50.191'W). Follow the main walk from ❹ (just after the 2h20min) point to the end and return as in the main walk.

Other short walks from the Refugio El Pilar: Users have written about two walks they enjoyed; these paths are shown on the map on page 99, but *not highlighted*. Both start by heading south from the *refugio* on the signposted GR 131. 1) After 45min turn off right on the signposted SL EP 104 and follow this down to a forestry road, then turn right and right again on the LP301 back to El Pilar. 2) After 1h stay left on the track (ignoring the path to the right followed in Walk 9); rise steeply in zigzags up a firebreak and then round **Montaña de la Barquita** and **Pico Birigoyo**, before descending to the *refugio*. And don't miss the short circular walk: Birigoyo — or **Ruta de los Volcanes 'lite'** on page 101, which also starts at El Pilar!

83

ndscapes of La Palma and El Hierro

This walk is a good introduction to La Palma. Your views stretch across both the eastern and western slopes of the *cumbre*, the island's mountainous spine. And how different those two sides are: the north is verdant with woodlands, the south an intrigue of volcanic splendour with a desert of black sand.

Alight from the bus at the large lay-by east of the old tunnel on the LP3, at a place called **Lomo de los Mestres**. To **begin the walk**, head south on the initially tarred FORESTRY TRACK (⭕) at the right of a tall electricity sub-station (bearing a mural depicting burnt trees, with a line underneath 'Y si fuese así?' ('And if this were to happen?'). Straight away you're engulfed by a dense mantle of trees and bushes. This evergreen forest, mainly composed of four types of laurel, covered much of southern Europe and North Africa some 15-40 million years ago. Unfortunately, little remains of this unique woodland, the Canary Islands and Madeira being its last refuge.

You snatch glimpses of San Pedro and some adjacent villages over the verdant slopes of the island's high eastern midriff. The only sounds will be birdsong and lizards torpedoing up the banks. After a gradual ascent you reach **La Pared Vieja**, a picnic area (❶; **1h45min**; Picnic 14a). Apart from weekends, when it is very busy, this cool, shady *zona recreativa* makes a good resting place. (A decade ago many of the pines here crashed down during storms or were felled; this pine, the *Pinus insignis*, was introduced by General Franco, but has proven too weak to stand the occasional winter storms on these islands because of its very shallow roots.)

First pass a track on the right, then a small building. Go straight ahead through the picnic area until you meet the El Pilar/San Isidro road (LP301). Don't follow it; instead, turn up to the right by a large information board and a sign, 'PARQUE NATURAL', and follow an old cobbled trail with yellow and white PR waymarks that passes above and to the left of the picnic area. Ignore small side paths and a track coming in from the left. Some 15m/yds further on you join a track coming from the right. At a junction of tracks two minutes later, keep straight ahead along a path. Cross the track and again rejoin the old path, as it ascends to the left. You pass a shrine on the right immediately. The *camino*

The Llano del Jable, a plain of pitch-black sand (Picnic 14c)

Valencia
EL PASO, LOS LLANOS
Centro de Visitantes
PR LP 1.1
PR LP 14
LP3
Cruce del Refugio
CUMBRE NUEVA
Cumbre Nueva
GR131
Lomo de los Mestres
SANTA CRUZ
0
1 km
0.5 mi
LP301
SL EP 100
SL EP 101
Mña de Enrique
1261
SL EP 102
PARQUE NATURAL CUMBRE VIEJA
Mña Quemada
1366
Pista Cumbre Nueva
Llano del Jable
SL LP 103
1505
1512
La Pared Vieja
PR LP 18
SAN ISIDRO
Refugio El Pilar
SL LP 104
El Gallo

climbs steadily, threading its way through the canopy of trees and shrubs.

Some 25 minutes up from the road, the path leaves the canopy of trees and widens out. At a small junction, turn left uphill on another path (**2**; signpost: 'REFUGIO DEL PILAR, PR LP 18'). Another junction follows: again keep left (SIGNPOST). Volcanic mounds begin appearing through the trees. A shallow V in the ridge leads you up to an earthen track — the **Pista Cumbre Nueva** (**3**; **2h20min**; SIGNPOST). Turn left along this track. *(The Short walk begins here, and Alternative walk 12-1 joins here.)* Then turn right down the El Pilar road (LP301), past the **Refugio El Pilar** picnic area (**4**; Picnic 14b).

Just opposite the main entrance to the *refugio* (which has a modest visitors' centre), turn right (sign on a tree, 'ACAMPADA', indicating a camping ground). Keep to the left of the showers and a shallow gully; after 50m/yds you will come upon a beautiful old waymarked path between the pines. After 15 minutes you come out of the trees into a stunning volcanic landscape, with magnificent views of the *caldera*. Cross the LP301 road (**5**; signpost: 'PR LP14, EL PASO, TACANDE') and continue on the path, beginning your descent to **Montaña Quemada** — the prominent grey-brown volcanic cone seen to your right.

When you meet the road again, don't follow it. Turn left onto the **Llano del Jable** (Picnic 14c) and follow the main track for 200m/yds, then turn right on another track (**6**; signpost: 'EL PASO, PR LP14'). After another 250m/yds, at a junction of tracks, turn right (**7**; signpost: PR LP 14, EL PASO; **2h50min**). Your path now crosses the tremendous lava flow from Montaña Quemada, which is just over 500 years old. On both sides are large lumps of volcanic rock covered in white and green lichen. After 10 minutes, near the end of Montaña Quemada, the path veers sharply left (SIGNPOST). Soon you reach the edge of the pine forest. The path does not enter it, but keeps following the lava downhill.

'Go with the flow' for the next 15 minutes, until the path gets steeper and zigzags down the lava, just before veering sharply right and leaving the flow. Climb for a minute, then continue downhill again. Ten minutes later, beautiful old stone walls appear on the right and a tremendous view opens up: the Cumbrecita in the distance and the Cumbre Nueva to the right. Some 50/yds further on, cross a track (SIGNPOST). The path is now flanked with old stone walls on both sides for the next 15 minutes. You pass a high fence and some houses on your right, and meet a road a minute later (**8**; SIGNPOST).

Follow the road to the right for 200m/yds and, at a signposted junction, descend the track straight ahead, lined with garden plots, orchards and some pretty houses. Ignore all side tracks and paths. When you meet the road again, turn left. Five minutes later turn right on a waymarked track (**9**; signpost: 'CENTRO VISITANTES CALDERA DE TABURIENTE'; **4h**). Pass a few houses and come into the lava stream again. In 10 minutes you reach the main road. The **Visitors' Centre** is opposite and the BUS STOP and a restaurant 30m/yds to the right (**4h10min**).

Walk 15: LOMO DE LOS MESTRES • LA PARED VIEJA • CUMBRE NUEVA • CAMINO DE LA FAYA • MAZO

Distance/time: 16km/10mi; 4h40min

Grade: 🔴 moderate, with an ascent of 450m/1500ft and descent of 950m/3100ft, much of it down an old cobbled path: *not recommended in wet weather, when it can be very slippery.* Yellow/white waymarking of the PR LP 17

Equipment: walking shoes (or boots), sunhat, sunglasses, suncream, raingear, fleece, windcheat, picnic, water

Transport: 🚌 Los Llanos bus *from Santa Cruz* (Línea 300) to the entrance to the *old* tunnel on the LP3; journey time 20min (see full details about this under 'Transport' on page 83). Return by bus to Santa Cruz (Línea 200 or 201; journey time 15min) or pick up a taxi when you reach Mazo.

Short walk: Circuit from La Pared Vieja (6.5km/4mi; 1h55min). 🔵 Easy-moderate; ascent/descent of 280m/920ft. 🚗 to the Pared Vieja picnic area on the LP301 south-west of San Isidro (28° 37.132'N, 17° 49.352'W). From **La Pared Vieja** follow WALK 15 on page 88 from ❶ to ❸, the LP301 by the **Pista Cumbre Nueva**. Then pick up the main walk below and walk the **Camino de la Faya** as far as 🔴. Turn left at this T-JUNCTION, then immediately right. The fairly overgrown track soon improves, and you descend gently, before joining the green/white waymarked SL BB 132 track to **La Pared Vieja**.

Highly recommended, this hike follows one of the finest old *caminos* (cobbled trails) on the island all the way to Mazo. It's called **El Camino de la Faya** (The Wax-Myrtle Trail), but in fact another tree is involved: the tree heath. The two often grow together in this northeastern part of La Palma. Called *fayal-brezal*, these woodlands create a transition between the *laurisilva* and the higher pine forests.

Start out by following WALK 14 on page 83 from the old tunnel entrance up to the 2h20min-point at ❸, where it briefly joins the **Pista Cumbre Nueva**. Just past here follow the El Pilar/San Isidro road LP301 uphill to the left. After 300m/yds, note a forestry track to the right called 'PF111 Llano de la Mosca'. Some 80m/yds beyond this track, turn left between two low stone walls (YELLOW/WHITE WAYMARKS), joining the **Camino de la Faya**. Soon a track comes in from the right and the path widens

Dense fayal-brezal is most common in northeastern La Palma near the Cumbre Nueva. You will also see it on other of the western Canary islands.

88 Landscapes of La Palma and El Hierro

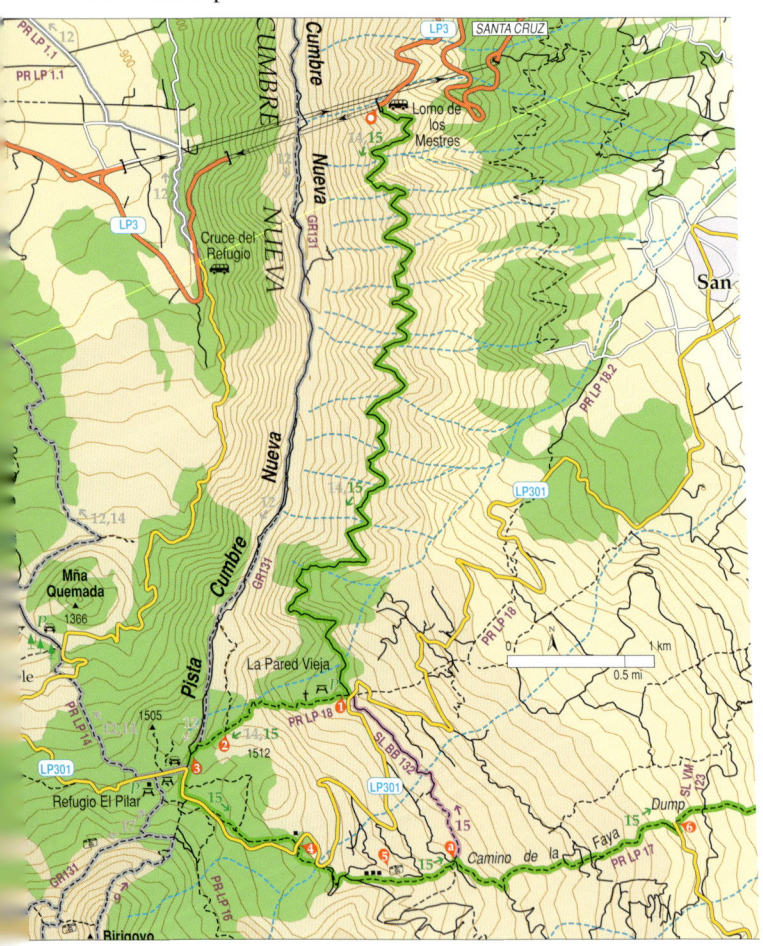

out. A couple of minutes along, turn right (SIGNPOST). Cross a track and, a few minutes later, cross the ROAD TO SAN ISIDRO by a building (**4**; **2h35min**; signpost: 'MAZO, PR LP 17').

Continue on the path that first veers sharply right and then left (by an enormous pine). After five minutes, join the MAZO TRACK. Turn right and, after 20m/yds, turn left down a path (SIGNPOST). Cross a wooden bridge and rejoin the track. Turn left and, after 170m/yds, turn left again (SIGNPOST; **2h45min**), immediately passing behind a shed, a house and another shed. Pass a VIEWPOINT (**5**) and, one minute later, at a junction, take the path going left (SIGNPOST).

Where the signposted SL BB 132 crosses your path, go straight on. Next, cross a minor track, only to rejoin it a minute later and follow it downhill. Another track now joins from the right. Almost immediately, at a T-JUNCTION (**6**), turn right

Walk 15: The Cumbre Nueva and the Camino de la Faya

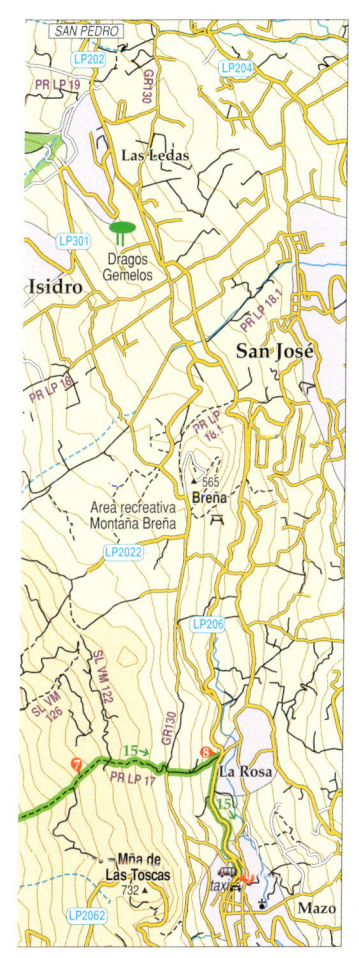

(WAYMARK). *(But for the Short walk, turn left here, back to La Pared Vieja.)*

Pass a signpost after a few minutes and after another few minutes descend to an intersection of four tracks, where you turn left on a path (SIGNPOST). Ignore any faint turn-offs or tracks until, after five minutes, you pass an APPLE ORCHARD and join a track (SIGNPOST). Follow the track to the right for 150m/yds, then turn onto the path again. The path crosses several tracks in the next 15 minutes (sometimes joining the track for 10 or 20m/yds; each junction is signposted or waymarked).

When the path eventually widens into a track, turn right down to the road to the old Mazo dump (SIGNPOST; **3h40min**). Turn left here and, when you reach the GATES TO THE DUMP (**6**), descend to the right on a path. At the next track crossing, turn left (SIGNPOST) to pick up the continuing path. Twenty minutes later, cross a track and then a covered *canal* (**7**). Just below the *canal* you join a track and follow it downhill, crossing another track a minute later (SIGNPOST).

The way finally joins a concrete lane, which you descend. On reaching a maze of country lanes, bear left after the third lane and descend a tarmac lane (signpost: 'PLAYA DEL HOYO, PR LP 17'). The tarmac ends shortly; continue straight downhill on concrete. Cross a minor track and continue on the steep concreted track to the left of a water tank. After a few minutes you arrive on the LP206 Mazo road in **La Rosa** (**8**; **4h25min**), just opposite a bus stop. Mazo is fifteen minutes along to the right. Keep right when you come to a fork in the road: the BUS STOP (**9**; **4h40min**) is just past the fork, and the taxi stand is a little further along.

...OS CANARIOS (FUENCALIENTE) • ...SAN ANTONIO • VOLCAN DE TENEGUIA • ...NCALIENTE

pages 2 and 20
...8km/5mi;
...16km/10mi; 4h20min if you return the same way)
Grade: ●❗ moderate, with a descent of 700m/2300ft on gravel slopes (steep and stony in places). You must be sure-footed and have a head for heights, but this walk is *recommended for everyone* (there is only one very short stretch that might prove unnerving for those who suffer from vertigo). It is usually very windy here, especially around the volcanoes. **Do not try to ascend to the rim of the Volcán de Teneguía in strong winds!** (when the authorities will close the path in any case). *Red and white GR waymarking for most of the way*
Note: There is a pay booth at the Volcán de San Antonio, €5 entry fee per person at press date; some walkers avoid this by going straight onto the path on the right, 100m/yds before the pay booth. If you avoid the pay booth, you will not be able to ascend to the rim of San Antonio.
Equipment: walking boots, sunhat, sunglasses, suncream, long trousers, cardigan, windcheat, raingear, swimwear, picnic, plenty of water
Transport: 🚌 from Los Llanos to Los Canarios (Línea 210); journey time 30min or from Santa Cruz (Línea 200 or 201); journey time 45min. Return on 🚌 from El Faro to Los Canarios (Línea 23); journey time 30min, then change to 🚌 to Los Llanos (Línea 210) or Santa Cruz as above (Línea 200 or 201).

Right: Roque Teneguía (top) and the Volcán de San Antonio, with Los Canarios in the background

Short walk: Volcán de San Antonio — Roque Teneguía — Volcán de Teneguía — Volcán de San Antonio (6km/3.5mi; 1h40min). ● Easy, but there is a stiff climb of 200m/650ft at the end. Equipment as above, but stout shoes will suffice. Access by 🚗: park at the Volcán de San Antonio. To get there, leave Los Canarios on the Las Indias road and, just past the last houses, turn left on a gravel track to the car park (28° 29.222'N, 17° 50.904'W), where a fee is payable. Follow the main walk from ❶ (the pay booth just before the 10min-point) to the 1h05min-point at the edge of the **Volcán de Teneguía** (❺), then return.

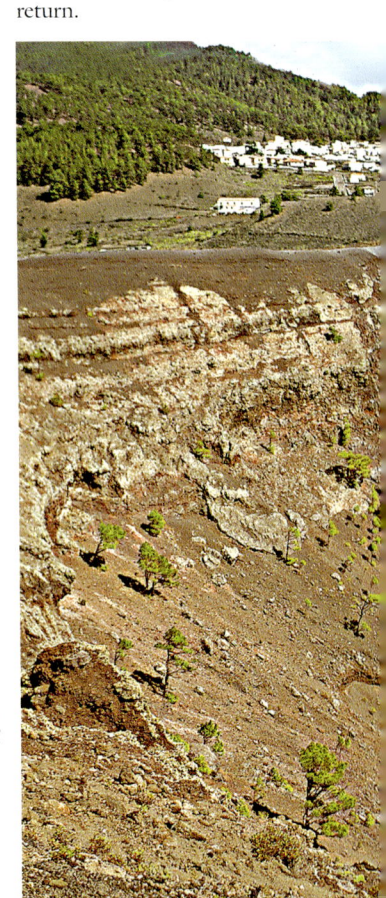

90

The Volcán de Teneguía is one of the most colourful volcanoes on La Palma, and the combination of striking coastal scenery and intriguing volcanic landscape make this a 'not to be missed' hike — and exceedingly popular. The walk ends at Faro de Fuencaliente, a working fishing hamlet.

Begin the walk at the **Bar Parada** in **Los Canarios** (⦿). ir's 200m/yds west of the BUS STOP on the main LP2 road). Walk down the narrow street opposite the bar. Go through a junction and reach the LAS INDIAS ROAD. Follow this to the right downhill and, after

TAZACORTE
SANTA CRUZ
LP2
810
800
LP2
Las Caletas
GR131
Mirador de las Indias
700
Las Indias
LP207
LP209
LP2091
Bodega Teneguía
16
Los Canarios (Fuencaliente)
Los Quemados
Bodega Carballo
Centro de Visitantes
667
Tablas
16
632
Volcán de San Antonio
500
300
200
100
Roque Teneguía
GR131
16
383
Montaña del Mago
444
226
Viento
400
427
Volcán de Teneguía
16
300
Mña de Lagi
219
LP207
LP207
GR131
16
Playa Nueva
Punta Malpais
Playa Enchentive
Salinas
Faro de Fuencaliente
Punta de Fuencaliente
0
1 km
0.5 mi

Above: descending to the lighthouse; left: at the beach

100m/yds fork right on a road, the CALLE DE LOS VOLCANES. (This fork is just beyond the turn-off for the Bodega Teneguía visited in Car tour 2.) You pass an *urbanización* on the right. Descending, you look straight onto the dark, flat-topped Volcán de San Antonio. Cross the Las Indias road again and head straight on for the crater. There is a PAY BOOTH (❶); the entry fee allows you to walk on the rim of the crater and visit the centre with a film about the Volcán San Antonio and Teneguía's eruption in 1971. There is also a good exhibition about vulcanism worldwide, so it's well worth a visit. (*The Short walk starts here.*)

Go through the VISITORS' CENTRE and onto the path at the right-hand side of the volcano (10min). A spectacular view opens up across hillside vineyards to Las Indias on your right; the sheer slopes of the western escarpment fill the backdrop, and you can see Puerto Naos, a handful of buildings backing onto a sea-flat of banana plantations. The crater rim is narrow in places, and some people may find a short stretch vertiginous. (Please don't lean on the 'safety ropes': you may end up in the crater...) Roque Teneguía is the yellow rock jutting out of the hillside below. The southern coast unfolds, with El Faro sitting near the southernmost tip, by glaring-white salt pans. But it's the magically-coloured Volcán de Teneguía that holds your gaze. It used to be possible to circle the whole of the **Volcán de San Antonio** CRATER (❷) on this path, but today it has been closed off halfway round for conservation reasons, so you will have to retrace your steps.

Return to the VISITORS' CENTRE, pass the pay booth and after 50m/yds turn left on a path (❸; signpost: 'FARO DE FUENCALIENTE, GR131'). A steep, gravelly and

Smooth rolling slopes on the descent to the lighthouse, on the stone-lined path

dusty descent brings you down to a track: turn left. Rounding the slopes, you look down on Roque Teneguía. Banana plantations and greenhouses vie to smother the coastal flat. Barely five minutes along the track, fork right on a clear path down to **Roque de Teneguía** (❹; **50min**). Although not large, this hunk of rock is a prominent landmark and a good viewpoint. While you are here, look out for petroglyphs; there are several of them on the sloping side of the rock, but they are quite faded. A barrier prevents visitors from clambering over this fragile rock and damaging the petroglyphs even more.

To continue, take the stone-marked path opposite the rock for less than a minute, climb down into a gully and walk down until you reach the *canal*. Turn left along the *canal*. Shiny-leafed *vinagrera* (of the dock family) flourishes here. After a few minutes, descend to a track seen below (to the left of a large WATER TANK) and follow it to the left, to where it joins the end of a track by a residents' parking area. Then take a path off right, to the EDGE OF THE **Volcán de Teneguía** (❺; **1h05min**).

(A path ascends to the left-hand RIM (●) of this spectacularly-coloured crater. It's a stupendous climb, *but narrow, vertiginous and very dangerous in a strong wind*. If it's calm and you make this ascent, add 20 minutes. Inside the crater, holes in the left-hand wall emit hot gases.)

The main walk continues by going back to towards the parking area, but shortly before it fork right on the continuing GR131, down into the lava. Keep between Teneguía and its offspring (a baby volcano) on the left. A clear stone-lined path soon leads you to a junction, where you turn right. Within minutes, at another junction, turn right again on a cleared path through an intriguing lava stream. The twisted and jagged rock here is spellbinding.

Out of the lava stream, your path crosses smooth rolling slopes. As you mount a crest, the pink-tinted salt pans and the lighthouse appear not far below. On arriving at the ROAD TO THE LIGHTHOUSE (❻; **1h35min**; SIGNPOST), turn right for 100m/yds, then pick up the continuation of your path on the left (SIGNPOST). A few minutes later cross the road again (SIGNPOST). Close to the edge of the cliffs, you look out over Playa Nueva, embraced by a lava flow.

Cross the road once more and descend to the tiny fishing hamlet of **Faro de Fuencaliente** (❼; **1h50min**). It's a desolate yet striking spot. Parched, windswept and covered in dust, you're just in the mood for a dip, then a cool beer and a reviving meal in the themed restaurant 'Jardin de la sal' right in the middle of the salt pans. There's a small but interesting MARINE RESERVE VISITORS' CENTRE here, too, in the old lighthouse (€2 entry fee at time of writing). There's a bus back to the village and a sign with the local taxi telephone number. Or allow 2h45min to return on foot.

Walk 17: RUTA DE LOS VOLCANES

Map begins below, ends on page 97
Distance/time: 18km/11.3mi; 6h10min
Grade: ●❗ fairly strenuous: while the ascent is only 500m/1600ft, the walk is very long, and much of it crosses volcanic gravel. Recommended only in fine weather: when the Cumbre Vieja is under cloud or mist, it's very easy to stray off the path, and *this could be dangerous*. Can be cold and windy. You must be sure-footed and have a head for heights. *Red and white GR waymarking; some green and white SL waymarking*
Equipment: walking boots, sunhat, sunglasses, suncream, raingear, fleece, windcheat, picnic, plenty of water
Transport: 🚕 taxi or with friends to the Refugio El Pilar (28° 36.845'N, 17° 50.191'W). Return on 🚌 from Los Canarios to Santa Cruz (Línea 201, journey 45min) or Los Llanos (Línea 210, journey 30min).
Shorter walk: El Pilar — Volcán Deseada — El Pilar (13km/8.1mi; 3h50min). Grade, equipment and access as main walk. Follow the main walk to ❺ (the 2h15min-point) and return the same way.
Other shorter walks from the Refugio El Pilar: see these suggestions on page 83.

Here's a walk to rival Tenerife's Cañadas or Lanzarote's Timanfaya. You go from one volcano to another, and each is more impressive than the last. Magnificent views lure you on, surround you, and trail behind you. By the time you reach Los Canarios, you'll have seen enough volcanoes to last a lifetime.

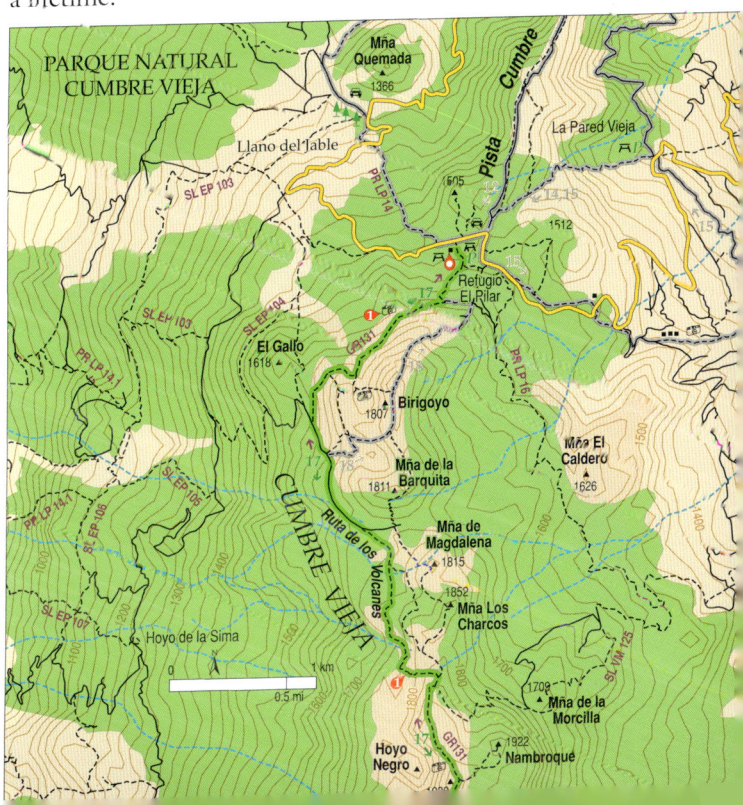

The walk starts by the VISITORS' CENTRE in the **Refugio El Pilar** picnic area (⬤; Picnic 14b). Some 50m/yds beyond (south of) this building, turn right on a path opposite a WATER TANK (signpost: 'LOS CANARIOS, GR131'). A steep ascent up through a pine wood follows. Under 10 minutes uphill, at a fork, keep right. Soon you're following a well-manicured path around the steep slopes of a volcano. Leaving the pines, a fine panorama unfolds at a *mirador* with a signboard (❶; **15min**): the hillsides slide down into the pine-studded basin cradling the Llano del Jable. Beyond these dark sands lie grassy fields, below the walls of the crater and the *cumbre*. El Paso spreads around the tail of a lava tongue, and Los Llanos is swallowed up amidst banana plantations.

Walk round the hillside, ignoring any paths ascending to the left Descend to a TRACK (**45min**; SIGNPOST). Turn left uphill, ignoring some minor tracks and paths. *(Walk 18 takes the*

Climbing above the Refugio El Pilar at the start of the walk

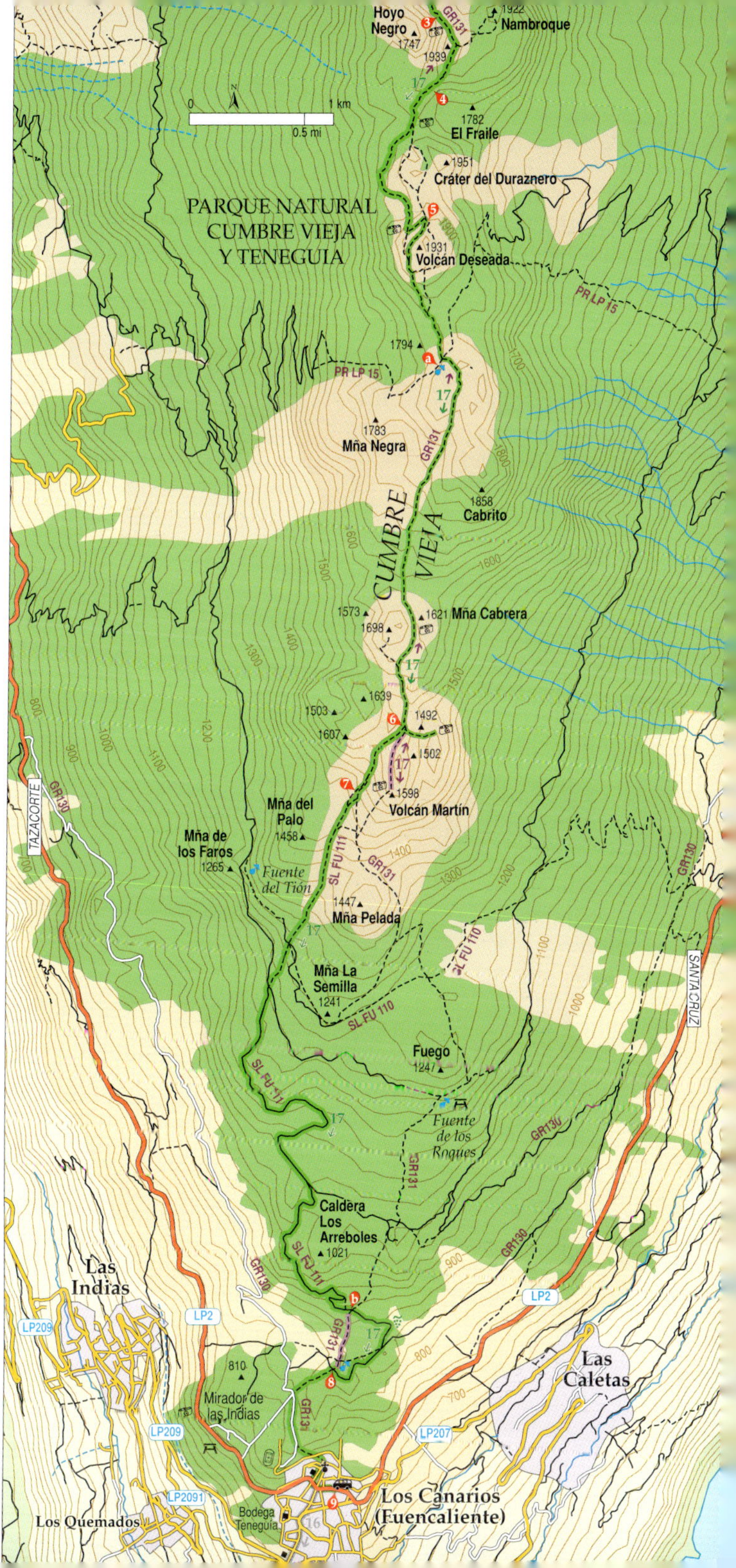

Hoyo Negro
1747
1922
Nambroque
1939
GR131
17
1782
El Fraile
1951
Cráter del Duraznero
0
1 km
0.5 mi
PARQUE NATURAL
CUMBRE VIEJA
Y TENEGUIA
1931
Volcán Deseada
PR LP 15
1794
1783
Mña Negra
1858
Cabrito
CUMBRE VIEJA
1573
1698
1621 Mña Cabrera
1639
1503
1492
1607
1502
1598
Volcán Martín
Mña del Palo
1458
Mña de los Faros
1265
Fuente del Tión
SL FU 111
1447
Mña Pelada
SL FU 110
Mña La Semilla
1241
Fuego
1247
Fuente de los Roques
GR130
TAZACORTE
SANTA CRUZ
Caldera Los Arreboles
1021
Las Indias
LP209
LP2
810
Mirador de las Indias
LP207
Las Caletas
LP2091
Los Quemados
Bodega Teneguía
Los Canarios (Fuencaliente)

cairned path soon passed, to climb to the Birigoyo summit.) Then, after 15 minutes, turn right on a wide path (initially flanked by stone walls; SIGNPOST), into a 'rock garden' of *codeso (Adenocarpus)* and chrysanthemums.

Cross a WOODEN BRIDGE (**2**; **1h20min**) and, a good five minutes later, ignore two paths to the left (SIGNPOST). After another 10 minutes' climbing, you reach a jagged-edged crater on the right. This is **Hoyo Negro** (**3**; the 'black hollow'), looking exactly like its name. Ten minutes later, you're peering down into a lava lake, the **Cráter del Duraznero** (**4**; **1h55min**). Descend to the right of this cone and, after a few minutes, at a fork, turn left uphill. (You will rejoin the right-hand fork further on.)

Just below the edge of the brilliantly-coloured **Volcán Deseada** (**5**; **2h15min**), the path forks to encircle it. Take the right fork. A minute later the crater tumbles away below you. Stay on the higher path halfway round the crater. A twin crater, to the left of the main one, emanates equally striking pastel hues — orange, pink, yellow and cream. (*The Shorter walk returns from here.*)

Leaving Deseada, you mount a neck of ridge, and ascend to yet another crater (**2h35min**). There are several paths to the rim of the crater — any one will do. This crater offers a spectacular view along the volcanic spine of its dark naked slopes. Swifts by the score whistle past. Bearing round to the right, you pass a CONCRETE POST. Just below the post, you rejoin the path that forked right just beyond El Duraznero. Continue straight downhill here. Leaving a shallow basin (SIGNPOST), you cross a low

Walk 17: Ruta de los Volcanes 99

crest. At a crossroads of paths (SIGNPOST; there is a WATER TAP 20m/yds to your right; ●) carry straight on. Entering a long shallow valley (**3h10min**), head across the sand and continue straight downhill (SIGNPOST); the odd survey post and stones intermittently line the path.

Soon (**3h45min**) the best views of the hike unfold (INFORMATION BOARD). The sea appears just over the edge of the sandy volcanic slopes, with the reddish-pink cone of Volcán Martín stealing the show. Luminous green pines dot the immediate hillsides. Within 10 minutes, at a major fork on the slopes of **Volcán Martín** (❻; **4h**; SIGNPOST), turn left. Turn left again at the fork that follows immediately. A minute downhill you're looking straight down into Volcán Martín, its rim ablaze with shades of mauve, cream and orange. Opposite, you can see a spring in a cave beside the crater floor. This is your last volcano, I promise.

Return to the forks and take the second left. (Or, if you're a glutton for punishment, take the first left, to ascend the crater rim and take in the extravaganza of volcanic hues shown below — as well as a good view over the southern tip of the island. Allow an extra 15 minutes for this.) Continuing, just head straight downhill, ploughing down through the fine gravel — great fun.

Just below Volcán Martín turn right at a fork, *leaving* the main GR131 path for the well-trodden SL FU 111 path with green and white waymarking (❼; signpost: 'FUENTE DEL TIÓN').

When you reach a TRACK (**4h35min**), cross it (signpost: 'LOS CANARIOS POR PISTA'). Then descend for a few minutes, to a junction (SIGNPOST). Take the track opposite and, from now on, just follow the signs for 'LOS CANARIOS' — going right at a fork after about 30 minutes (signpost: 'LOS ARREBOLES, FUENCALIENTE'). (After about 55 minutes the track crosses the original GR131 footpath to Los Canarios. If you decide to take this short-cut (●), turn right here. After three minutes cross another footpath and after another few minutes cross the track to continue along the path, rejoining the main walk.)

Attention is needed around an hour down the main track

'Gluttons for punishment' can take a 15-minute detour along the rim of Volcán Martín to enjoy this extravaganza of volcanic hues.

(**5h40min**), when you are circling to the right of a vineyard. Just before it, ignore a minor turn-off left. After a few minutes a track joins you from the left. Ignore the signposted path to the right, and continue on the track towards Los Canarios. A few minutes later, keep an eye out for a WATER TANK on the right. Some 30m/yds past the tank, turn left on a path (**8**; signpost: 'GR131') and follow it straight downhill, picking up red and white waymarking again.

On reaching a road, follow it to the left (SIGNPOST). Soon you pass a basin with pines and see a sports field in the distance. Where the road veers right, take the path to the left (SIGNPOST). Los Canarios comes into sight just below, through the trees. On meeting the road again, cross it and continue on the path (SIGNPOST). Emerging on a street in **Los Canarios** (**6h05min**), follow it 100m/yds downhill to the MAIN ROAD. Turn left and walk past Bar Parada (where Walk 16 begins). The BUS STOP is just three minutes further on; a bus shelter is opposite (**9**; **6h10min**).

View to the Caldera de Taburiente from the summit of Pico Birigoyo (Walk 18)

Walk 18: BIRIGOYO, OR RUTA DE LOS VOLCANES 'LITE'

See photos opposite and on page 96
Distance/time: 4.5km/2.8mi; 2h15min
Grade: ● moderate, with an ascent/descent of 350m/1150ft on gravelly, loose rock and sand; you must be sure-footed. *Red and white GR waymarking at the start*
Equipment: walking boots, sunhat, sunglasses, suncream, raingear, fleece, windcheat, picnic, water, walking poles
Transport: 🚕 taxi or with friends to/from the Refugio El Pilar (28° 36.845'N, 17° 50.191'W).

This short, but very pretty walk, with tremendous views, is the best option if you don't have time or stamina for the whole Ruta de los Volcanes. The Birigoyo summit affords a splendid outlook — not only over the Caldera de Taburiente (see opposite), but across the island to both coasts and along the Ruta de los Volcanes — all the way to Deseada.

Start out at the VISITORS' CENTRE in the **Refugio El Pilar** picnic area (○). Follow WALK 17 on page 100 past the **Mirador de Birigoyo** (❶; 15min) and until you join the track (45min). Follow this for a few minutes until, just after a rugged lava flow, you can turn left on a FAINT PATH MARKED WITH CAIRNS (❷). In seven minutes you reach the rim of a pretty crater full of pines. Turn left uphill; after another seven minutes you reach the RIM of **Birigoyo** (1h05min) and look into the impressive crater.

Now turn right on another cairn-marked path which rounds the crater on the south side. You enjoy tremendous views to the south, east and west. If the weather is clear, this is where you will see both coasts. Climbing higher, then round the crater towards the north, ignoring some minor paths to the right and always keeping to the crater's rim.

From the SUMMIT of the volcano (❸; 1h30min) you enjoy the uninterrupted view over the Caldera de Taburiente shown opposite — better than from any vantage point on the Ruta de los Volcanes.

From here head northeast over the ridge *(do not turn left)*. A steep zigzag descent over rubble follows, past a smaller crater on the right. On reaching the first shrubs (1h45min) the path veers to the right and zigzags down into the forest (1h55min). Five minutes later, first ignore a small trail to the left, then turn left down a wide FIREBREAK (❹), ignoring a track on the left. Just 100m/yds further down another track crosses the fire break; follow this to the left. It narrows to a path. Keep straight on: you meet your outgoing path a minute later. Follow it to the right for less than 10 minutes, back to the **Refugio del Pilar** (2h15min).

Walk 19: PICO BEJENADO

Distance: 13.5km/8.4mi; 4h25min
Grade: ●❗ strenuous, with an ascent/descent of 830m/2720ft, but suitable for anyone who is reasonably fit. You must be sure-footed, and a few stretches demand a head for heights. Only suitable in fine weather; should clouds descend, the utmost care needed, especially at the summit. If a strong wind is blowing, keep away from rim of the crater. Signposting and yellow/white waymarking (PR LP13.3).
Equipment: walking boots, sunhat, sunglasses, suncream, raingear, long-sleeved shirt, long trousers, fleece, warm jacket, gloves, picnic, plenty of water
Transport: 🚗 car to/from El Barrial, above Valencia. Turn off the El Paso/ Santa Cruz LP3 road for 'Parque Nacional' (at the Visitors' Centre). Keep straight on at the first junction but, shortly after, turn left for Valencia. Keep ahead on this road for 3.3km and park when it reverts to rough track (28° 40.581'N, 17° 50.960'W). Another parking area lies further up this track, at the point where the ascent proper begins and the road is once again surfaced; you may prefer to park there if you are in a 4WD vehicle.

Pico Bejenado, like Pico de la Nieve, is accessible to everyone, and for this reason alone, worth the effort of the ascent. You'll feel like an eagle once on the summit, as you peer down into every corner of the Caldera de Taburiente (Walk 20). And on the ascent you have a sweeping vista over the Los Llanos basin as it spills out into the sea. This hike offers a superlative of views.

These timings begin at the point where the asphalt *first* ends (**○**; signpost: 'PR LP13,3 BEJENADO'). Follow the track ahead to the turn-off left for the ascent, by a large park INFORMATION BOARD and a second parking area with SIGNPOST (**❶**; **20min**). At a junction (**❷**; **35min**) go left ('PICO BEJENADO, POR PETROGLIFO, 4900M'). Ignore a wide path ascending to the right just past this junction. The hillsides are wooded in Canary pines and bare of undergrowth. Pico Bejenado is the peak furthest to the left in the wall of mountains ahead.

Another SIGNPOST (**❸**; **1h**) points your way up a wide path to the right. (A curiosity: there's a rubbish bin here with braille lettering.) Minutes up, the path narrows and zigzags. A little over five minutes later, keep left at a fork (**❹**; signpost: 'PETROGLIFOS 150M'). But it's worth taking the short detour to right, to see the large petroglyph at ● and take in the excellent views over the mountains near La Cumbrecita.

The ascent steepens as you mount the shoulder of the crater, but the panorama expands to encompass the west coast, where a gentle built-up plain fans out from the basin of fields tucked back into the *cumbre*. Ignore a path to the left (**1h35min**).

Soon, at **El Rodeo** (**❺**; **1h45min**), the rim of the crater is just before you. Go left (SIGN-POST); the path to the right leads to La Cumbrecita. The far walls of the pine-speckled *caldera* below you may well be under a mantle of clouds, which only enhances the picture (as in the photo below).

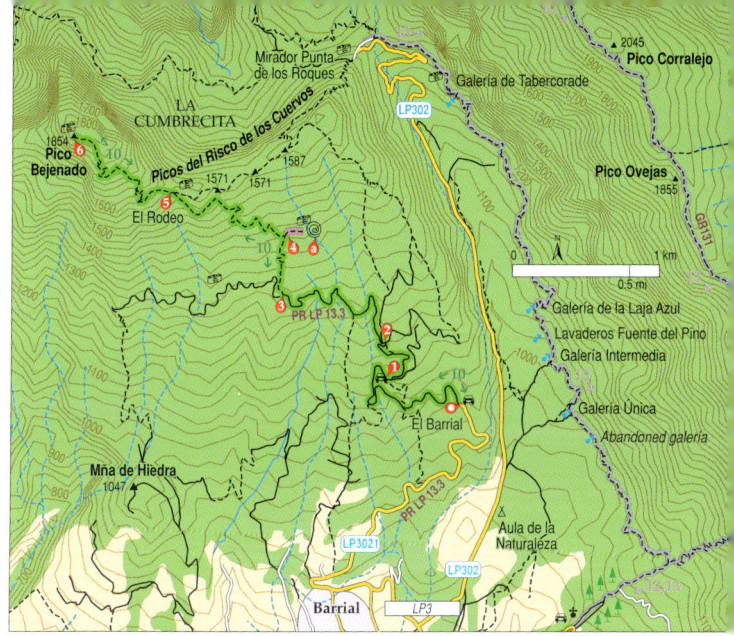

Finally, you reach the SUMMIT of **Pico Bejenado** (**6**; **2h25min**), with a bird's-eye view over the whole crater, lined by streams of ridges pouring down off the encircling wall of mountains. The strip of *barranco* bed visible below is the Playa de Taburiente. If you scramble down the 2m/6ft-high rock-face on the west side of the summit and continue to the end of the ridge, you will be able to look down into the Barranco de las Angustias and trace the forestry track up its far wall to Los Brecitos, where Walk 20 begins.

Retrace your steps to the LOWER CAR PARK (**4h25min**).

At the summit of Bejenado, with a bird's-eye view of the whole crater

Walk 20: CALDERA DE TABURIENTE FROM LOS BRECITOS

See also photos on pages 24-25 and 110-111
Distance/time: 12.5km/7.8mi; 5h
Grade: ●❗ long and quite strenuous, with a descent of 850m/2790ft, but accessible to all fit walkers who are sure-footed and have a head for heights. ***Don't attempt in bad or windy weather, or after heavy rain:*** conditions change every year in the *barranco* after heavy rainfall, with a danger of rockfall or (very rarely) flash flooding. The going also depends on how much water the *barranco* is carrying, making the walk easier (usually in summer) or more difficult (usually in winter). Other hints: It can be very cool: be prepared! And don't lean on any handrails: they may be loose.
PR LP13 signposting; yellow/white waymarking
Important notes: Permission is needed from the Parques Nacionales if you intend to stay in the national park overnight (obtain this at the Visitors' Centre on the LP3, or telephone 922-922280 or book online at http://www.reservas parquesnacionales.es), and you may camp *only* at the designated site. *Please don't follow the watercourses in this crater, as suggested in some books: they are too dangerous — tourists have died as a result.*
Equipment: walking boots, sunhat, sunglasses, suncream, raingear, long-sleeved shirt, long trousers, fleece, warm jacket, gloves, swimwear, picnic, water, walking stick. It's a good idea to leave a dry pair of shoes, socks and trousers in your car or backpack, especially in the winter, in case you slip while crossing the river!
Transport: 🚗 car or taxi to/from the parking area in the floor of the Barranco de las Angustias (see Car tour 3, page 24), then jeep taxi to Los Brecitos (they wait here for walkers; shared cost is about €12-13 per person). *Note:* the taxis only operate from 08.00-13.00 in summer, 08.00-12.00 in winter.

The Caldera de Taburiente *is* La Palma. If you don't spend at least a day in it, you haven't really seen the island. Streams tumble down from every *barranco*; indeed, these streams formed the *caldera* (cauldron), which at first was thought to be volcanic. Some nine kilometres (six miles) across at its widest point, and 2000 metres (over a mile) deep, Taburiente is one of the largest craters in the world to be formed by erosion. Recent studies, however, shy away from the crater theory, claiming it to be a massive landslide instead. It's one of La Palma's three natural wonders (the other two being the Ruta de los Volcanes and Los Tilos).

The walk starts at the car park in **Los Brecitos** (⭕): descend the path by a large NATIONAL PARK SIGNBOARD, pass through a turnstile, and head down into the *caldera*. Follow the path signposted 'ZONA DE ACAMPADA', ignoring all turn-offs. Hillsides tumble away below, and the rocky crater walls tower overhead, with pines clinging to the sheer slopes. *The pine needles can be very slippery underfoot!* You cross a number of small *barrancos*, some with

Right: not far below Dos Aguas

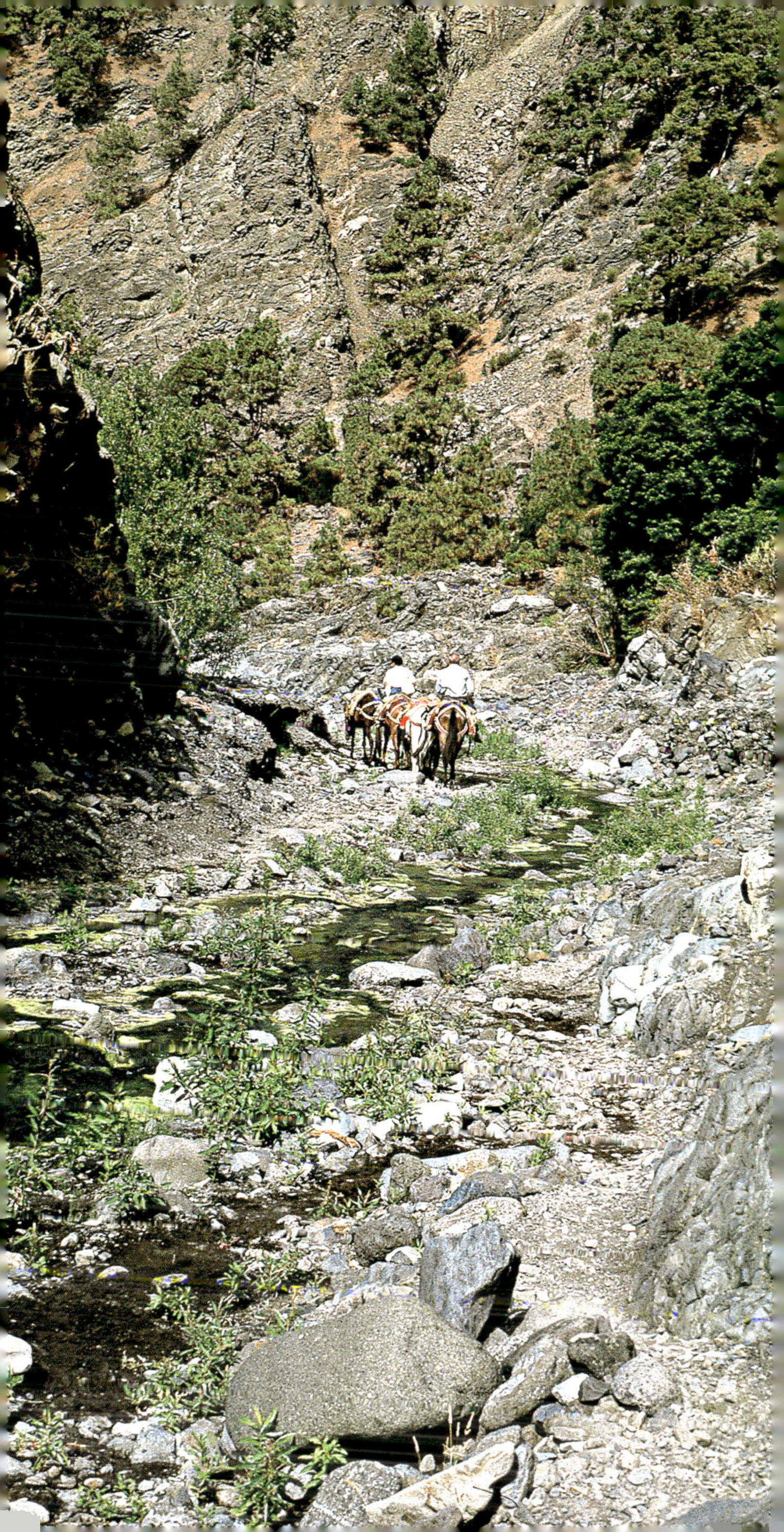

106　Landscapes of La Palma

streams. The prominent peak rising out of the *caldera* wall opposite is Pico Bejenado. Walk 19 goes to its very top.

A large boulder marks your crossing of the **Barranco de las Traves** (❶; **35min**). More boulders begin appearing on the hillsides. The next ravine, the **Barranco de las Piedras Redondas** ('ravine of round rocks'), is well-named. The **Mirador del Lomo de Tagasaste** (❷), from where you have a good view into the centre of the crater, follows. The deeply-gouged ravine of the **Barranco de Bombas de Agua** (❸; **1h15min**) will either impress you or terrify you, or both, as you continue along the path! Erosion here eats away at least a couple of feet from the *barranco* walls every year.

You finally arrive at the floor of the **Río Taburiente** at a wide basin known as the **Playa de Taburiente** (❹; **1h25min**). Here you're enveloped by grand scenery. Small clumps of cool, shady Canary willow (*Salix canariensis*) stretch along the wide stony *playa*, where you can paddle in smaller or larger pools with crystal-clear water.

To continue to the camping site, cross the river, hopping over boulders and stones, and look out for a gap in the willows on your right approximately 50m/yds downstream (SIGNPOST; WAYMARK), to locate the path that ascends the eastern bank of the river to the CAMPING SITE above (❺; **1h30min**). There is an attractive stone-built services centre here (information and toilets).

Keep to the left of the buildings (SIGNPOST); follow a wide path over to the edge of a cliff with a wonderful view straight

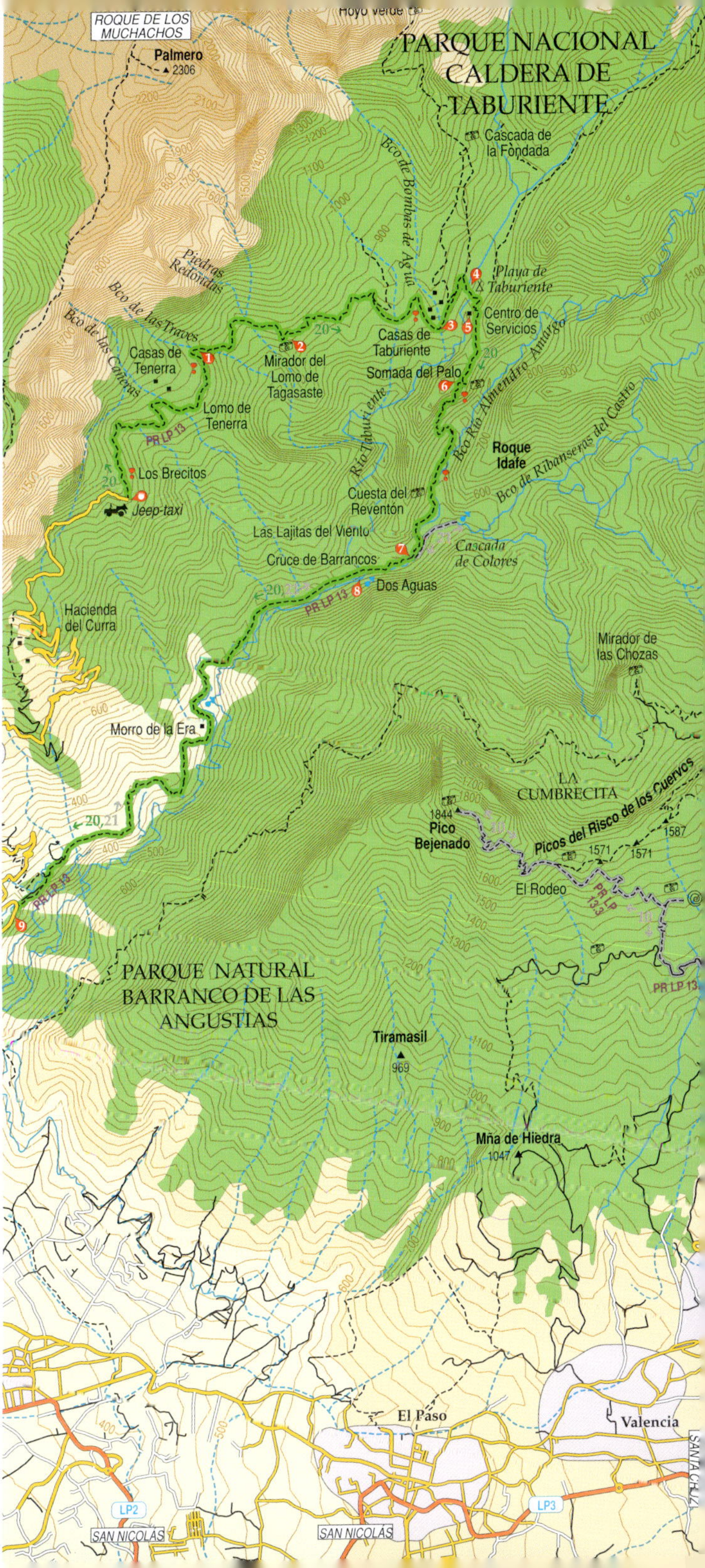

ROQUE DE LOS MUCHACHOS
Hoyo Verde
Palmero
2306
PARQUE NACIONAL CALDERA DE TABURIENTE
Cascada de la Fondada
Bco de Bombas de Agua
Piedras Redondas
Bco de las Traves
Bco de las Cañeras
Playa de Taburiente
Centro de Servicios
Casas de Taburiente
Bco Río Almendro Amargo
Casas de Tenerra
Mirador del Lomo de Tagasaste
Somada del Palo
Lomo de Tenerra
PR LP 13
Río Taburiente
Roque Idafe
Bco de Ribanceras del Castro
Los Brecitos
Jeep-taxi
Cuesta del Reventón
Las Lajitas del Viento
Cruce de Barrancos
Cascada de Colores
Dos Aguas
Hacienda del Curra
Mirador de las Chozas
Morro de la Era
LA CUMBRECITA
Picos del Risco de los Cuervos
1844
Pico Bejenado
1571
1587
El Rodeo
PR LP 13.3
PARQUE NATURAL BARRANCO DE LAS ANGUSTIAS
Tiramasil
969
Mña de Hiedra
1047
El Paso
Valencia
SANTA CRUZ
LP2
LP3
SAN NICOLÁS
SAN NICOLÁS

down to the Río Taburiente. The path continues over a col and soon Roque Idafe comes into sight, a prominent finger of rock balancing on the end of a ridge.

The **Somada del Palo** (**6**; **1h45min**), a signposted viewpoint on a nose of hillside jutting out into the plunging **Barranco del Río Almendro Amargo** ('bitter

Walk 20: Caldera de Taburiente from Los Brecitos

almond'), provides a fine perch over the river and equally good views back up to the heights of the crater. After about 30 minutes' descent on the partly-cobbled, winding path, look back up the *barranco* for a good view of a wall spanning the ravine. At the fork that follows five minutes later, keep right. A few minutes later the path that branched off to the left rejoins your route at **Las Lajitas del Viento**, from where you continue downhill.

Another signpost (**7**; 'LAS ANGUSTIAS/ZONA DE ACAMPADA; **2h25min**), marks the confluence of two streams, the **Cruce de Barrancos**. *(Walk 21 heads into the river here, to the 'Cascada de Colores'.)* We keep right and continue along the path, reaching the river bed in five minutes. There is usually a fair amount of water here all year round, as no water is collected at this point. Hop across as best you can — with a bit of luck you'll keep dry! Soon you arrive at **Dos Aguas** (**8**; **2h40min**), the confluence of the Almendro Amargo and Taburiente gorges. There is a giant grate on the left here, to collect debris from the river where it flows into a *canal*. Cross the **Río Taburiente**, then pick up the continuing path (at the left of a low concrete wall built across the **Barranco de las Angustias**; signpost: 'BARRANCO DE LAS ANGUSTIAS, SALIDA'). Continue downstream along this *barranco*.

The time spent in the *barranco* greatly depends on your agility, as you scramble over rocks and jump across the river. Depending on the amount of water the river carries, you may have to leave the stream bed several times. All seven diversions are signposted with green boards, but the signs are rather high up the ravine walls and easily missed. The first detour, to the left, is just after a large pipe crosses the *barranco* above your head (at about **3h10min**). The second comes up about five minutes later, also on the left-hand wall. The third is also on the left. The fourth is on the *right-hand* wall. (Of course it is usually possible to stay in the bed of the *barranco*, getting your feet wet!)

Eventually you arrive at **Morro de la Era**, a derelict stone building (**3h50min**). After returning to the *barranco* for five minutes, there's another detour up the left wall, then you descend once more to the *barranco* bed (**4h15min**). Before crossing the stream again from here, head *upstream* for two minutes, to a delightful pool and cascade hidden in a rocky corridor under a natural rock arch — most hikers miss this spot. After a sixth detour up the right wall, continue in the stream bed, which eventually dries up (in summer). A seventh detour is to the left just before the car park, but it is not usually necessary to follow this one. When you arrive at the main track your car will be in the PARKING AREA a couple of minutes along to the left (**9**; **5h**).

Left: looking up the Barranco de Ribanseras del Castro from just below its confluence with the Río Almendro Amargo (Cruce de Barrancos)

Walk 21: BARRANCO DE LAS ANGUSTIAS AND THE CASCADA DE COLORES

See also photos on pages 24-25, 105 and 108
Distance/time: 11km/6.8mi; 4-5h
Grade: ● Moderate, with an ascent/descent of some 250m/820ft; much clambering over rocks and some paddling. *Don't attempt after heavy rain:* after heavy rainfall, there is a danger of rockfall or (very rarely) flash flooding. The going also depends on how much water the *barranco* is carrying, making the walk easier (usually in summer) or more difficult (usually in winter). PR LP13 signposting; yellow/white waymarking. See also 'Important notes' at the top of page 108..
Equipment, Transport: as Walk 20 on page 108. Park in the Barranco de las Angustias (28° 41.144'N, 17° 54.570'W)
Short walk: *Barranco de las Angustias* (up to 5.5km/3.4mi; 1h50min). Grade, equipment, access as main walk. Follow the walk to ❶, **Morro de la Era** (an ascent/descent of about 130m/425ft) — or turn back any time you like.

This walk is a bit shorter and less strenuous than Walk 20, and you will not have to rely on the jeep taxis or wait for them to fill up, but can head off at your own pace. There are no vertiginous spots either, but you will still have to flounder in the river bed! The highlight is the 'waterfall of colours' — on everybody's 'bucket list' — but the entire expedition is splendid.

To begin from the PARKING AREA in the floor of the **Barranco de las Angustias** (**O**) follow the yellow/white PR LP13 waymarking and 'ZONA DE ACAMPADA' signposting, to climb the bed of the *barranco*. Remain in this *barranco*, ignoring all side-*barrancos* off to the left. The route, very well signed and waymarked, eventually follows a *canal*, then crosses it and passes the **Morro de la Era** (❶; 1h10min), a ruined hut.

In the setting shown on page 105, we reach a dam at **Dos Aguas** (❷). The path rises at the left of the dam, to the CONFLUENCE of the **Río Taburiente** and the **Barranco Río Almendro Amargo**. Crossing the Río Taburiente, ignore the path left to Playa de Taburiente (Walk 20 descends this path) at **Cruce de Barrancos** (❸; 2h), the

Left: boulder-hopping in the Barranco de las Angustias, not far from Morro de la Era; right: the orange-yellow rocks at the Cascada de Colores owe their colour to the iron content in the river (clearly visible in the photo on page 108).

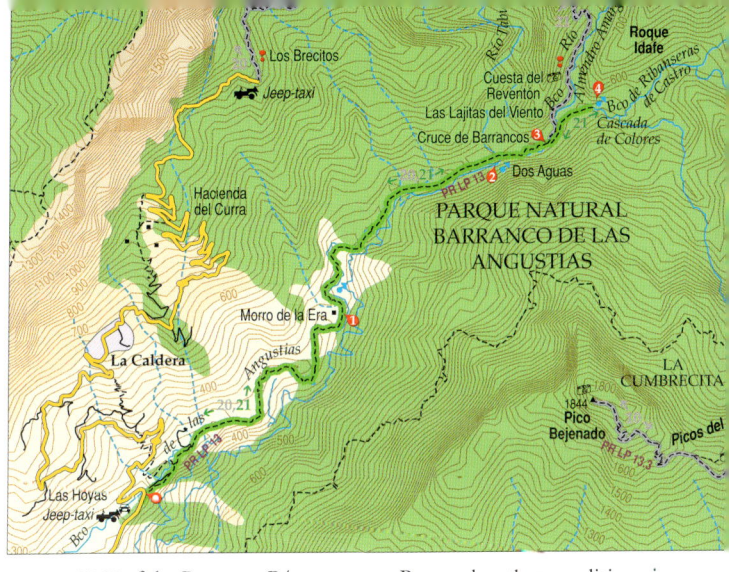

CONFLUENCE of the Barranco Río Almendro Amargo and the **Barranco de Ribanseras de Castro**. You're now in the setting shown on page 108.

Keep right now in the Barranco de Ribanseras. Notice the rust-coloured water, caused by the high iron content. You will have to cross this stream several times on loose slippery rocks; the last two minutes are awkward and need care. Remember that conditions in the *barranco* change every winter and you may have to paddle and or clamber over landslides to get to the waterfall. In 15 minutes you should arrive at the 'coloured waterfall' (**Cascada de Colores**; ❹; **2h15min**), a brilliant sight.

Return the same way from the cascade, but remain in the bed of the *barranco* if you can, when it is carrying little water.

Walk 22: FROM THE MIRADOR EL TIME TO PUERTO DE TAZACORTE

Distance/time: 3km/2mi; 1h
Grade: ●❗ easy but steep descent of 600m/2000ft; not suitable in wet weather. You should have a head for heights, but the path is generally quite wide. *Red and white GR waymarking*
Equipment: walking boots, sunhat, sunglasses, fleece, water, bathing things
Transport: 🚌 bus from Los Llanos (Línea 110) to the Mirador El Time; journey time 25min. Return on 🚌 from Puerto de Tazacorte to Los Llanos (Línea 27 or 110); journey time 15min.

This walk is one long, continuous panorama. The vista stretches out over the Los Llanos plain and along the west coast to the south of the island. It's a short walk, ideal for late afternoon, and a great 'appetiser' for beginners.

Set out from the **Mirador El Time** (◯), but first take in the superb panorama at this viewpoint. Small volcanic cinder cones stand out on the inclines, speckled with white houses, and banana plantations stretch for as far as the eye can see. The cliffs below you plunge down into the Barranco de las Angustias before it cleaves its way into the Caldera de Taburiente (Walks 20 and 21).

Walk downhill on the narrow road on the northwest side of the restaurant and souvenir shop (SIGNPOST). The hillside below you is stepped in banana groves all the way to the sea-cliffs. When you reach the EDGE OF THE CLIFFS (**5min**) an even more expansive view unfolds, all the way up the Barranco de las Angustias and into the Caldera de Taburiente.

A few minutes later, the trail leads through walled-in banana groves. Leaving the groves on a rough track, go right to round the hillside, following the good GR waymarking. Another few minutes along, turn left downhill, to join a road and descend amidst greenhouses. Descend to a T-junction and turn left (❶; **20min**; signpost: 'GR131 PUERTO DE TAZACORTE').

Follow the road to the left, past park-sized gardens ablaze with colour and some ritzy homes enjoying a stupendous view. Three minutes down the road, turn left down a concrete ramp (SIGNPOST) which becomes a nicely cobbled path. After a few minutes on this path, flanked by high walls, the path joins the road again, by an old

From the old cobbled camino real you have a superb view over Puerto de Tazacorte spectacularly located at the mouth of the Barranco de las Angustias.

banana-packing station, before continuing down left (SIGNPOST).

Now you are walking into a picture-postcard. You edge the rim of the plummeting **Barranco de las Angustias**, peering down onto Puerto de Tazacorte. From up here you can appreciate its beautiful location at the mouth of the *barranco*. On reaching the sea-cliffs, the way twists and winds down the sheer face of the escarpment. Don't walk *too* near the edge, as the cliffs drop away without warning ... you might do the same! The descent is made even more impressive because of the beautifully-made path underfoot — an old cobbled *camino real* (**2**), which descends in zigzags. Offshore you can see some large fish cages (fish farming), and the colourful village lies below you in the mouth of the *barranco*.

About half way down the cliffs (**40min**), the route veers left across the wall of the *barranco*. A bit further down you pass a number of once-inhabited caves, now barred up to prevent hippies from using them. You finally approach **Puerto de Tazacorte** from behind banana groves (beware of broken glass here). Walk along the promenade for 100m, then turn left on a walkway which rounds the sunken plaza. Then bear right to the BUS STOP (**3**; **1h**) on Avenida del Emigrante, south of the ROUNDABOUT in front of the Casa del Mar restaurant.

Walk 23: TIJARAFE • PORIS DE CANDELARIA (THE 'PIRATES' COVE) • TIJARAFE

Distance: 8km/5mi; 3h05min
Grade: ●❗ very strenuous, with a descent/re-ascent of 650m/2100ft. You must be sure-footed and have a head for heights. Don't attempt in wet or windy weather. Although people *do* swim at Poris de Candelaria, I would not generally recommend it because of the swell. *Inconsistent yellow and white PR waymarking, as well as cairns on the footpath*
Equipment: walking boots, sunhat, sunglasses, suncream, fleece, raingear, swimming things (just in case the sea is mirror-calm), picnic, plenty of water
Transport: 🚌 from Los Llanos to/from Tijarafe (Línea 110); journey time about 35min. Or 🚗: park in Tijarafe (28° 42.684'N, 17° 57.357'W) and make your way to the Supermercado San Antonio and the kiosk on the main LP1 road.
Alternative return to Tijarafe: After visiting Poris de Candelaria, go back to ● (the 1h10min-point) and take the NARROW CONCRETE ROAD back up to Tijarafe. Timing is approximately the same, but the ascent is easier.

Poris de Candelaria is an exquisite little hideaway. Supposedly, it was once used for just that purpose by pirates. Although there is a motorable lane down to this little cove, most drivers would find it far too hair-raising. If you're really fit, a far better way to get there is on foot, following this brilliant, if strenuous walk.

Start out in **Tijarafe**. From the BUS STOP, cross the street, walk uphill to the SUPERMERCADO SAN ANTONIO (**O**) and the little KIOSK next to the *ayuntamiento* (town hall) and take the road between them. Passing between the GUARDIA CIVIL and the CENTRO DE SALUD, the street narrows into a concrete lane and descends steeply, flanked by terraced plots.
At an INTERSECTION (**❶**; **10min**), turn right on a track. Three minutes along, ignore a gated track running back to the right. Ignore another track off right 300m/yds further on, as you round the top of the **Barranco de la Cueva Grande**. After another 250m/yds, in a tributary, a partially cobbled path crosses. Turn left here (**❷**; **25min**) — this is the PR LP 12.2, but waymarks are scarce, so *watch carefully* now for the small CAIRNS that waymark the route; this crest is criss-crossed with goat paths — all of which look like potential footpaths! The path will lead you down the ridge between the Barranco del Pueblo on the left and the Barranco de Cueva Grande on the right. Lone pines dot the grassy inclines, and a mixture of vegetation grows out of the grass: *tabaiba, taginaste, vinagrera, verode* and prickly pear.
You cross the Barranco de la Cueva Grande below a DRY CASCADE (**❸**; **40min**). As the path zigzags down the steep slopes, inexperienced hikers may find it unnerving, although it is amply wide. Loose stones and gravel make this steep descent slippery,

Right: the 'pirates' cove', where weekend retreats are built into the massive rock overhang

114

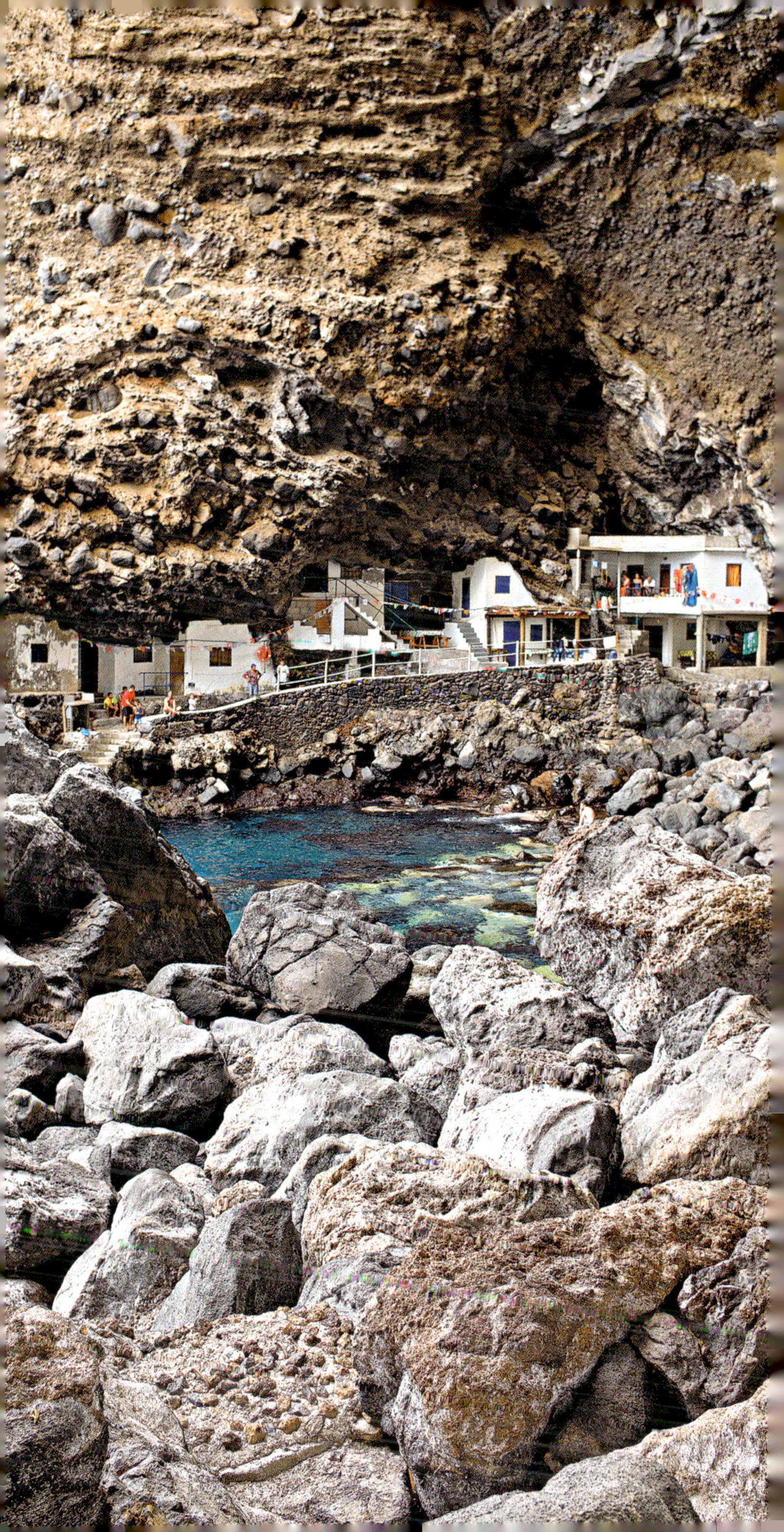

A wide path leads to the cove. Only swim here if the sea is mirror-calm!

so take your time. A number of small CAVES (④) lie beside the path; nearer the shore many have been converted into sheds or even dwellings. At one point the path passes very close to the top of a cliff from where there is an excellent VIEW (⑤) across the plunging sea-cliffs to the north-west coast. Large clumps of the cactus-like candelabra spurge begin appearing on the seaward slopes.

A path coming from the narrow concrete road and parking area joins your path (●; **1h10min**), and from here a good wide path takes you down into the hidden cove, **Poris de Candelaria** (⑥; **1h15min**). Rounding the point, the most unexpected sight appears: an enormous shallow sea cave towers overhead. Weekend retreats, dwarfed by the 50m/150ft-high overhang, huddle around its base, just at the edge of this tiny inlet.

The bad news is: the homeward leg is 1h50min of sweat and tears. The good news is: when you reach **Tijarafe** (**3h05min**), beer will never have tasted better!

116

Walk 24: FROM TIJARAFE TO TINIZARA

Distance/time: 5.3km/3.3mi; 2h15min
Grade: ● easy-moderate, with ascents of about 350m/1150ft overall. *Red and white GR waymarking all the way*
Equipment: walking boots, sunhat, sunglasses, suncream, fleece, raingear, picnic, plenty of water
Transport: 🚌 from Los Llanos (Línea 110); alight one stop beyond Tijarafe village; journey time about 35min. Return on the 🚌 same bus from Tinizara; journey time about 45min

My hiking companions call this the 'friendly hike', and so it is. Following bits and pieces of the *camino real* along the cultivated western shelf of La Palma, you seem to pass through everyone's back garden. The proud old cobbled trails weave their way amidst terraced plots of almond trees and dip into ravines in between them.

In the bus push the button, or shout 'Para aquí por favor', just after you pass the main part of the village of **Tijarafe** and a big bend in the road. **The walk begins** just northwest of the BUS STOP, some 50m/yds uphill from SUPERMERCADO CANDELARIA (●). Turn left down a road and then take the first right, heading through fields of almond trees with strips of vineyards and clumps of prickly pear in their midst. After two minutes, when the road swings left, turn right on a track (signpost: PUNTAGORDA, GR130, CAMINO REAL DE LA COSTA). Then turn left on a cobbled trail, rejoining the road a minute later (SIGNPOST).

Now follow the road downhill. Palm trees begin appearing, dotting the landscape. The terrain is very rocky, with many ravines concealed in the inclines. After two minutes, when the road curves left to descend the **Barranco del Aserradero** (❶; SIGNPOST), turn right to climb the ravine on the old *camino*.

Soon (**10min**), flanked by an extravaganza of flowers, opposite a house, you meet a road. Cross straight over onto a path flanked by a high stone wall. Round the hillside on a clear path through almond groves, ignoring side paths. Seven minutes past the house, ignore a fork to the right, and immediately cross the **Barranco de la Cueva Grande** (❷). Climb a splendid piece of old trail, and then emerge on a road, at a bend. Turn left downhill (SIGNPOST).

At a junction two minutes down the road (where there is a WATER TANK on the left), keep straight ahead on a concrete track (**25min**; SIGNPOST). Pass a SHRINE on your right and, 50m/yds further on, come to a house. Continue to the right of this house, surrounded by other beautiful, newly-built houses. Now the descent begins into the picturesque **Barranco del Pinillo** (❸), where there is a gigantic rocky protrusion in the ravine wall and a large house built partly in the rock. Not far downhill, turn left on a path (SIGNPOST) and follow it down to the floor of the *barranco*. Creepers drape the ravine walls. On your ascent up the other side, both abandoned and 'done-up' houses lie along the route.

Cross another (tiny) stream bed and soon pass a beautifully restored house (❹; **45min**). Just after it, you come onto a lane. About 100m/yds along the lane, turn left on a tarmac drive which narrows to the *camino real* once more and passes a couple of small orchards. Don't forget to look back occasionally, over the green hillsides descending to the sea, speckled with dark soldier-straight pines. In the distance lies the chain of volcanoes that punctures the island's southern spine.

Walk 24: From Tijarafe to Tinizara 119

Above: the attractive 19th-century house with a shrine. Left: the ascent from the Barranco de la Baranda to Tinizara is the most picturesque stretch of the walk.

Coming to a T-junction, turn left, pass a house on the left and continue along the *camino*. Ignore a concrete lane coming in from the right. Tarmac comes underfoot briefly, then the *camino* heads left and crosses a *barranco*. Joining the lane again, after a little over 100m/yds a SIGNPOST points you right on a cobbled path. Small stone dwellings sit partially hidden in the rocky terrain, camouflaged by clumps of prickly pear cactus. Note the white powder on the prickly pear. It's the cochineal parasite (photo page 126), once collected for its scarlet dye.

After a minute along this 'short-cut', you're back on the lane (**1h15min**; SIGNPOST). Pass tracks to your left and right, and pass the charming early 19TH-CENTURY HOUSE (**5**) shown above (on your right). Notice the shrine in the wall. A minute later the GR130 turns off left for another 'short-cut' — only to bring you to the lane again three minutes later. Follow the lane for under 100m/yds, then branch off right (SIGNPOST).

Climb up the hill on his beautiful old footpath and, when you meet the lane again 10 minutes later, cross it. Soon you reach a VIEWPOINT (**6**) at the edge of a big ravine, the **Barranco de la Baranda**. The trail drops you down into a chasm — the deepest of them all, and a fine shady place to picnic. Cross a STREAM BED (**7**) overgrown with blackberry bushes.

From here, the way to Tinizara

is a steep climb, but the most picturesque section of the walk, up the fine old trail shown below (ignore all side-paths; continue straight up). Almonds wood the terraced hillsides. Just below the lane (**2h05min**), you pass a handful of houses — some traditional, some new, some renovated. Cross the lane (SIGNPOST) and continue on the path. A minute up, reach the lane again. Follow it to the left. After two minutes, turn up a wide path to the LP1 (SIGNPOST). The BUS STOP in **Tinizara** (❽; **2h15min**) lies 50m/yds to the left. The local bar is a minute further along.

Rising up the camino *to Tinizara*

Walk 25: EL FAYAL • LAS TRICIAS • CUEVAS DE BURACAS • LAS TRICIAS

Distance: 8km/5mi; 2h35min (2h05min for motorists)
Grade: ●❗ relatively easy, with a descent of 400m/1300ft and ascent of 300m/1000ft. You must be sure-footed and have a head for heights. Not recommended in wet weather. *Red and white GR waymarking, also some local signposts*
Equipment: walking boots, sunhat, sunglasses, suncream, fleece, picnic, plenty of water

Transport: *No convenient buses. Either* 🚌 Línea 120 from Barlovento to the turn-off for the El Fayal *zona recreativa* just before Puntagorda (journey time 1h25min) or 🚌 Línea 110 from Los Llanos (journey time 55min). Return on 🚌 Línea 120 from Las Tricias to Barlovento. *Best by* 🚗: park in Las Tricias (28° 46.865'N, 17° 57.794'W) and use the map to join the walk at the church, saving 30min.

Las Tricias is known for two groups of residents — arboreal (the unique assembly of dragon trees) and human (the transient 'alternative life-stylers'). Both have become noteworthy curiosities in themselves, attracting tourists in droves. To avoid the crush, finish this walk before midday, and you'll be able to share the sights with just a few other people.

Begin the walk from the BUS STOP AT THE TURN-OFF FOR EL FAYAL (❍): continue northeast along the road towards Las Tricias. The surrounding slopes are wooded in Canary pines. Three minutes along, you'll see an INFORMATION BOARD and GR signposting for SANTO DOMINGO at the side of the road and a small white SHRINE below you, on the edge of the Barranco de Izcagua. Take the path down past the shrine and into the *barranco* (signposting: 'LAS TRICIAS'). The path sidles down the sheer escarpment, where some guard rails lend psychological support *(but don't lean on them!)* A stand of pine trees fills the valley floor. Ten minutes down, the way swings left and enters the bed of the **Barranco de Izcagua**. Five metres further on, the path leaves it again, to ascend the right-hand bank.

Mount the crest, greeted by a grove of almond trees. Continuing along the edge of the *barranco*, pass through a gate (please leave it as you find it) and ignore a few entrances to fields on the right (**25min**). A minute later, on joining a concrete lane, turn left (❶; signpost: 'EL FAYAL, PUNTAGORDA, GR130, CAMINO REAL DE LA COSTA'). Some 20m/yds downhill, turn right on a track (signpost: LAS BURACAS, ST DOMINGO). When this track ends, the old path becomes your way again, lined at the left by small country dwellings. Crossing a small *barranco*, you gain a first view of some large dragon trees on the hillside above.

This scattered little quarter of **Las Tricias** retains much of its original character. As you pass between some old homes with traditional high windows, chickens and cats scatter in all directions.

Emerging from the houses, you descend to the LAS TRICIAS ROAD (❷; SIGNPOST; **40min**), below the village centre. Cross a smaller road going left here and make your way down the main road to the right. A

121

little over five minutes down the road, just before it curves to the right, take the first cobbled lane on the left (signpost: LAS BURACAS, ST DOMINGO). It passes between two houses, and you come onto a track. Two minutes down the track, you pass through an intersection, and asphalt comes under foot. Just past the first house on the right, take the cobbled path descending to the right (signpost: 'RT TRAVIESA'). A minute down, opposite a house named LA CASA BLANCA, rejoin the road and follow it downhill for just over 100m/yds. At this point, where the road bends right, turn left on a track running along the edge of Barranco de Izcagua, *ignoring* for now the signposted GR path (**3**) at the very beginning of this track (it is the return route). The track quickly peters out into a narrow path. Keeping straight down, pass rustic cottages set amidst colourful gardens and fruit trees. Although the hillsides are cultivated, they have a dishevelled appearance. More dragon trees appear.

Reach the ROAD (**4**) and turn left, making for an old windmill standing on the hilltop ahead, by following the road to the left, then ascending a chained-off track on the right. The WINDMILL (**5**; **1h05min**) has an adjacent museum dedicated to *gofio*, which certainly merits a visit. A good vista awaits you as well: the ridges flatten out on their descent before finally dropping into the sea. The ridge to the north is the refuge for the island's biggest concentration of dragon trees. Humble cottages lean up against the rocky ridge.

From here return the short way to the road junction where you turned left to visit the mill (**4**). Turn left and follow this road for just under 200m/yds, to regain the COBBLED GR PATH (**6**; SIGNPOST). Turn left, cross a track in a couple of minutes, and descend past some superb dragon trees. Follow the beautifully cobbled path as it descends the crest of the ridge and takes you past more dragon trees.

Your next stop is the Buracas Caves, soon to be seen in the far wall of the *barranco* to the right. A good ten minutes down the ridge on this manicured path (ignoring turn-offs), you pass some low cottage rooftops on your left. At a T-JUNCTION (**7**) 50m/yds further on (signpost: 'BIO CAFÉ FINCA ALOE'), turn right and round the wall of the *barranco*. At the next junction, near this café-bar (which offers lovely light refreshments and health food), go right again.

In a few minutes you're standing in front of the **Cuevas de Buracas** (**8**; **1h30min**). The main cave is really just an overhang of

The windmill and museum at Las Tricias, where you can learn about gofio *and its importance to the Canarian diet*

Walk 25: Around Las Tricias 123

rock. It's not much to look at, but a short way up the path beyond it there are a few more (equally unspectacular) caves, and some rocks marked with petroglyphs.

Now return to the ridge and ascend it, keeping to the crest. In 25 minutes you reach a track (*SIGNPOST*). Cross it (and the adjacent *canal*) and continue up a cobbled path. You cross a road a minute later — back at ⑥ (*SIGNPOST*). Heading up through almond trees, you walk under a massive dragon tree. Joining another track, turn 3m/yds left to the road and follow this back up to *LA CASA BLANCA*, now on your right.

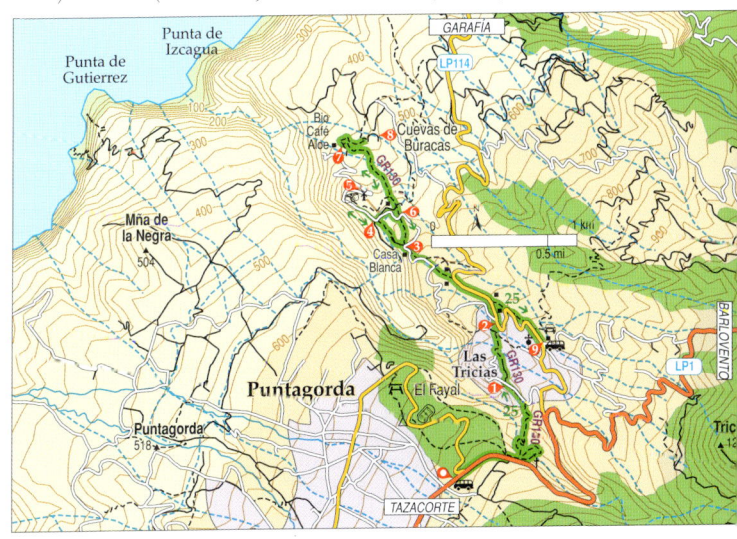

124   Landscapes of La Palma and El Hierro

Ascend the cobbled path opposite, and return along your outward route. Once back on the LAS TRICIAS ROAD (**2h15min**), 100m/yds short of where you first joined it at ❷, follow it uphill for five minutes, until you see a concrete lane ascending between two houses on your left. Climb the lane and rejoin the road. Some 100m/yds up the road, turn left on another concrete lane ascending the hillside, probably with a couple of crabby little dogs at your heels. You rejoin the road just 150m/yds below the village shop/bar in **Las Tricias**; follow the road up to the left, to the BUS STOP (❾; **2h35min**) in front of the village shop.

Dragon trees at Las Tricias. The white powder visible on the prickly pear is the cochineal parasite, which used to be collected for its scarlet dye.

Walk 26: GARAFÍA • EL PALMAR • JUAN ADALID • EL PALMAR • GARAFÍA

See also photos on page 156
Distance: 13km/8mi; 4h05min
Grade: ●❗ moderate, with ascents/descents of 400m/1300ft overall. Some short stretches demand a head for heights. Not recommended in wet weather. Can be extremely windy. *Red and white GR waymarking; yellow/white PR waymarking in the first 30 minutes*
Equipment: walking boots, sunhat, sunglasses, suncream, warm jacket, raingear, picnic, plenty of water

Transport: 🚐 from Barlovento to/from Garafía (Línea 120); journey time 1h10min. The bus stops at the Casa de Cultura at the village entrance. Or 🚗: park in Garafía near the *plaza* (28° 49.787'N, 17° 56.706'W).
Short walk: Garafía — El Palmar — Garafía (6.3km/3.9mi; 1h40min). ●❗ Easy, with ascents/descents of 200m/650ft overall. Otherwise grade, equipment and access as main walk. Follow the main walk to **El Palmar** (❸) and return the same way.

The north of the island remains relatively untouched by tourism. Being far from the main tourist centres, it hasn't become a hiking highway like the Ruta de los Volcanes or the Caldera de Taburiente. It's wild and rugged, with villages few and far between.

Start the walk at the Garafía BUS STOP (❍), at the turning for the village centre. Walk straight to the *plaza* (main square). The church shown overleaf is worth a visit if you have the time (see touring notes on page 18). Then locate the **Mirador el Chorro** (❶) behind the church, where the trail begins. (It's opposite a strange three-storey building, the old pharmacy, and there's a large, confusing sign here in three languages: read the part for the GR130.)

Follow the small road uphill past the *mirador* for 50m/yds, then turn left with the GR130 on a cobbled path descending into the **Barranco de la Luz** (signpost: EL PALMAR, BARLOVENTO, GR130, CAMINO REAL DE LA COSTA). First you'll notice the dragon trees. Large clumps of the cacti-like candelabra spurge grow out of the *barranco* walls too.

The path crosses the bed of the *barranco* (❷) and climbs out the far side (this ascent may be unnerving for those who have no head for heights). You pass a number of caves with goats and two houses built into the hillside, and emerge on the end of a CONCRETE TRACK (**10min**). Keep ahead on the track for two minutes, then turn right on a path. Two minutes later, back on the track (no longer concreted, but with a SIGNPOST), turn right but, after under 20m/yds, pick up the old *camino* again, below the track (SIGNPOST). You go through two wooden gates; please close them behind you. You round the hillside, passing through traces of terracing. Open and spacious, devoid of settlement and with windswept vegetation, this is La Palma's 'wild (north)west'. Soon the rocky shoreline comes into view.

Passing above an uninhabited homestead, descend to a track and follow it to the right for 10m/yds. Then pick up the path again, straight ahead — in places it's a beautifully built old stone-laid trail. Solitary houses dot the sides of ridges. The terrain is rocky; little grows here except for the usual xerophytic vegetation. Ascend to a narrow road (**35min**; SIGNPOST) and follow it downhill to the left. Two minutes down, turn right to rejoin the old path. Two minutes further along, when you are overlooking a homestead, the way forks. Take the right fork. The *barranco* here is full of candelabra spurge.

On the bend just before the homestead, ascend the path to the right (signpost: DON PEDRO), walking alongside a small *casita*. A few renovated and derelict cottages lie below. This is **El Palmar** (❸), and soon you arrive at the edge of the deep **Barranco El Palmar** (**50min**). *(The Short walk returns from here.)*

Now descend into the ravine. Approaching the floor of the *barranco* (❹), keep left. Then walk along the stream bed to the right, to a *fuente* (spring) hidden behind enormous yam leaves. The water is refreshingly cool but, unfortunately, the spring is dry in summer.

From the *fuente* return along the *barranco* bed for 10m/yds, where your path out of the *barranco* ascends to the right. Climbing the wall of this ravine, you pass several caves. A stiff climb takes you up to a COUPLE OF BUILDINGS (❺; **1h10min**). Pass above them and, two minutes later, walk behind another house. Don't forget to enjoy the view behind you: a pleasant feeling of isolation spreads over these hills. A minute later you join a minor, unused track. The few houses you can see strung out along the edge of the *barranco* opposite comprise the hamlet of El Mudo, now virtually abandoned. A few minutes along, the path joins a minor track: keep

The palm-lined plaza and 16th-century church of Nuestra Señora de la Luz in Garafía

left (SIGNPOST). The tops of wind generators now appear over the crests of the ridges ahead. Some five minutes later, you come to the MAIN TRACK (**6**; **1h25min**) that descends to El Mudo (signpost: JUAN ADALID, BARLOVENTO). Follow this track to the right uphill for a minute, then rejoin your path (SIGNPOST). The surrounding hillsides are covered in cistus and heather.

One final, deep ravine follows — the **Barranco Domingo Diaz**. A blade of ridge jutting into the sea below, surmounted by a chapel, catches your attention on this fairly vertiginous, but amply wide path. Amazingly enough there's a track up to the chapel. At the bottom of the *barranco* (**7**; **1h55min**), as you are entering an enclosure, please leave the GATE as you find it.

Climbing out of the *barranco*, the way is blocked by fences and another gate. Go through the gate (again leaving it as you find it) and follow the path through a 'tunnel' of heather. Beyond the heather and past a house, you look across a shallow gully onto a couple of farm houses dwarfed by two giant wind generators. Quite a sight! Cross a farm track, and dip into the gully, ignoring the turning to the left.

Passing to the right of a house, the path arrives at a road in an area called **Juan Adalid** (**8**; signpost: DON PEDRO, BARLOVENTO). Turn left downhill, then turn left again on the track to the WIND GENERATORS and climb the HILLOCK beyond them (**9**; **2h10min**). If there isn't a gale blowing, this is the perfect spot for a picnic. A couple of lonely outposts lie on a coastal shelf below. Looking across the northern coastline, severed by sheer cliffs, the village to the east is Gallegos (Walk 1).

From here retrace your outward route back to **Garafía** (**4h05min**).

WALKS

Photo: the Arbol Garoé, or Arbol Santo

El Hierro

Walk 27: FROM THE PISTA AL DERRABADO TO SABINOSA

Distance/time: 6.5km/4mi; 2h05min
Grade: ● ❗ quite easy, with a descent of 600m/2000ft. You must be sure-footed and have a head for heights on some short sections. Don't attempt in wet weather. It can be very windy and cold on this walk, and the *cumbre* is often covered in cloud. *White/yellow PR waymarking most of the way*
Equipment: stout walking shoes, sunhat, sunglasses, suncream, long-sleeved shirt, long trousers, jacket, windcheat, raingear, picnic, water
Transport: 🚗 taxi or with friends to the Pista al Derrabado (27° 44.356'N, 18° 2.883'W). Return on 🚌 from Sabinosa (Línea 7); departs 15.45 Mon-Fri; 14.10, 19.30 Sat/Sun/hols; or telephone to Tigaday for a taxi from the bar in Sabinosa

Alternative walk: Pista al Derrabado — Fuente de Mencáfete — Pista al Derrabado (10km/6.3mi; 3h30min). ● Moderate, with an overall ascent/descent of about 340m/1115ft. Gentle track walk, but the final path to the *fuente* is steep and slippery. Access by 🚗 as above; wear walking boots. Follow the main walk to ❸, at which point stay on the track. This climbs in wide bends. Ignore the PR EH 1.2 joining from the right (●) and continuing uphill about 100m/yds further on — it's easier to avoid as much of this steep path as possible. After about 25 minutes the track ends and a steep, narrow signposted path continues another 80m/260ft up to the **Fuente de Mencáfete** (●; **1h45min**) — two small round basins high in the valley.

This walk, on a lovely forestry track above the Golfo crater, is ideal for beginners. It takes us into the Reserva Natural de Mencáfete, home to fine examples of *fayal-brezal* and *laurisilva* (see page 87). In fact the laurels up at the Fuente de Mencáfete (Alternative walk) are some of the most beautiful on the island — but that involves a tricky path.

Start the walk at the junction with a track, the **Pista al Derrabado** (○; signpost: 'FUENTE DE MENCAFETE'). From here you have a splendid view across the banana and pineapple plantations of El Golfo to the rocky islets of Salmor. **Set off** by following this track: it gradually descends around the sheer face of the escarpment, into the **El Golfo** crater. The hills are thickly wooded in laurel. The western part of the crater is bare of life save for the veins of stone walls that cross it. A spa, the Pozo de la Salud, is marked by a prominent hotel standing above the sea.

At one point (**35min**) you have an uninterrupted view through a gap in the vegetation over the

View to Sabinosa on the descent

western wing of the crater. Pass through farmland set on shelves high in the wall of the *cumbre*. A good 20 minutes later, a path (the PR EH 1) joins you from the left. Some 200m/yds further on, where an asphalt road goes right, keep left for 'FUENTE MENCAFETE'.

Around five minutes uphill, an ENCLOSED PROPERTY sits off the track to the right (**1h**). Just beyond it, be sure to leave the track, taking a grassy, perhaps overgrown path downhill (signpost: 'SABINOSA, PR EH1'). Five minutes later, a path goes left to Fuente de Mencáfete (Alternative walk). Round a steep hillside; you will keep to this path all the way to Sabinosa: ignore any minor paths turning off.

A stone bench with a sign, 'KING'S STONE' (**Piedra del Rey**; **1h20min**) makes a good rest stop. Just past it, as you round a bend, a bird's-eye view unfolds down onto the picturesque but rather severe looking Sabinosa, atop a volcanic mound that protrudes from the crater wall. The dark volcanic slopes that surround it are patched in vineyards. The descent of these gravel slopes may prove slightly unnerving for some. When you reach a street in **Sabinosa** (**2h**) keep straight ahead to Camino la Dehesa. Then go right downhill on Calle Hoya del Moral. The bus leaves from the *plaza* (**2h05min**); the local bar is to the right.

Walk 28: SABINOSA • MIRADOR DE BASCOS • EL SABINAR • ERMITA DE LOS REYES • SABINOSA

See also photos on pages 1 and 131
Distance/time: 14.2km/8.8mi; 5h25min
Grade: ●❗ very strenuous, with an overall ascent of about 900m/2300ft. You must be sure-footed and have a head for heights. Don't attempt in wet weather. It can be very windy and cold on this walk, and the *cumbre* is often covered in cloud. *White/yellow PR waymarking throughout, also some red/white PR waymarking*
Equipment: walking boots, sunhat, sunglasses, suncream, long-sleeved shirt, long trousers, jacket, windcheat, raingear, picnic, plenty of water
Transport: 🚐 (Línea 12) or 🚗 to/from Sabinosa; motorists should park near the *plaza* (27° 44.861'N, 18° 5.887'W)
Alternative walk: Sabinosa — Ermita de la Virgen de los Reyes — Sabinosa (8.5km/5mi; 3h35min). ●❗ Very strenuous, with an ascent of 650m/2100ft. Grade, equipment as main walk. Access by 🚐 (Línea 12) or 🚗 to/from Sabinosa (motorists park as above). Follow the main walk to **Las Casillas** (❶). Cross the track here; then, 100m/yds further on, ignore a track off to the right. Some 15 minutes along, take a rough track descending to the right (the GR131, **Camino de la Virgen**; signposted). When you reach the **Piedra de los Regidores** at junction of tracks, pick up the main walk again at ❹ and follow it to the end.

L a Dehesa, the island's pastoral highland, is an enchanting landscape, often enveloped in teasing fog and mist. This walk visits several highland beauty spots, starting from the pristine village of Sabinosa. We climb to splendid views over El Golfo, then to the protected Sabinar and the famous Virgen de los Reyes chapel.

Start the walk at the WALKERS' INFO BOARD and SIGNPOSTS by the *plaza* in **Sabinosa** (⭕): walk up **Calle Hoya del Moral** on the yellow/white waymarked PR EH 1. At a fork 100m/yds along, keep right. Then, just where the trail begins to descend, turn left uphill on a well-maintained path signposted 'CAMINO A LA DEHESA'

Ermita de la Virgen de los Reyes

Walk 28: Circuit from Sabinosa to La Dehesa

(the yellow/white waymarked PR EH 9.2).

A steep zigzagging climb through vineyards and then heather follows, with no turn-offs to worry about. Dark green junipers dot the lower inclines. Don't forget to enjoy the views behind you. On reaching the tree-heather and evergreen zone, you may well be enveloped in cloud — notice the rocks and tree trunks beside the path, thick with moss. Nearing the *cumbre* the way is slightly vertiginous. This is where you feel the full brunt of the wind, too.

Just over the CREST, by a SIGNPOST, you meet the end of a track on the edge of the **Dehesa** highland at a place called **Las Casillas** (❶; **1h15min**). You over-look a pastoral landscape here, littered with old lichen-clad stone walls. Some 50m/yds further on, at a fork, turn sharp right downhill on another trail, the PR EH 9 at the edge of the El Golfo crater.

The trail moves away from the edge of the basin, and after 10 minutes or so you go through a GATE. You leave the pasture walls behind as you walk to the left of a small pine wood making a half-hearted attempt to forest this uneven basin. But these pines are out of the wind and, with luck, in the sun — as idyllic a spot as you'll find on the island. Ten minutes from the gate you meet a crossing track: turn right here, to the **Mirador de Bascos** (❷; **2h25min**). What a view! You look straight down on Sabinosa and the

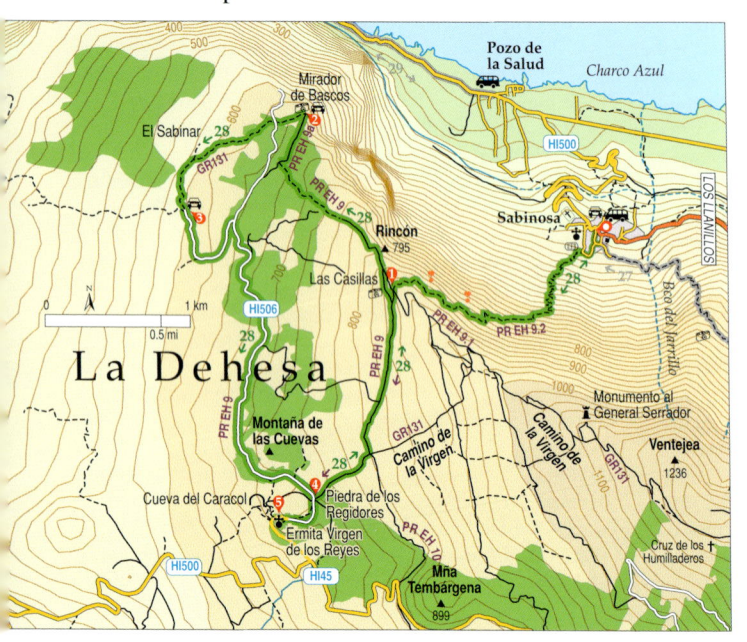

Pozo de la Salud and, if it's not in cloud, the view extends over the whole El Golfo basin to Las Puntas.

From the car park here at the *mirador* turn half right downhill with the signposted PR EH 9. You cross a motorable track and 15 minutes later pass a viewpoint at the right of the trail, on the far side of a wall. Already you can see the wind-buckled junipers *(sabinas)* below at El Sabinar. Now the trail descends beside the wall to the **Sabinar** CAR PARK (❸; **2h45min**).

Leaving El Sabinar, follow the track out: in about 15 minutes it rejoins the track from the Bascos viewpoint. Turn right, and keep to this main track. Half an hour or so later, you pass through a GATE as you round the richly red **Montaña de las Cuevas**. Then you come to the **Piedra de los Regidores** (❹) at a junction of tracks. Every four years, the July 'Bajada de la Virgin' begins here at dawn. Take the third track to the left here, the red/white GR131), which cuts through an old crater. Five minutes along, turn left down a paved walkway to the **Ermita de la Virgen de los Reyes** (❺; **3h40min**).

From the *ermita* retrace your steps to the **Piedra de los Regidores** (❹), then take the signposted 'CAMINO DE LA VIRGEN'; it's waymarked yellow/white for the PR EH 9 and also red/white for the GR131. In 10 minutes you come to a crossroads, where you turn left with the PR EH 9 on a track. Keeping straight ahead, in some 25 minutes you'll be back at **Las Casillas** (❶). From here retrace your steps down the zigzag path to **Sabinosa** (**5h25min**).

Walk 29: COASTAL WALK AT ARENAS BLANCAS

Distance: 4.5km/2.8mi; 1h10min *by car*; 9.5km/6mi; 2h20min *by bus*
Grade: ● easy, flat; *recommended for everyone*. The path is far enough away from the waves to be safe, but spray (especially from blowholes) may reach the path on a rough day: *care with children!* And *do not leave the path:* the coastline itself is crumbly and unstable.
Equipment: walking shoes, cardigan, water

Transport: 🚗 to/from the signposted 'Arenas Blancas' parking area on the HI500 (the 14.6km-point in the car tour; 27° 45.964'N, 18° 7.573'W); at times this low-lying road is closed after storms. Or 🚌 (Línea 12; convenient departures/returns; see timetable page 157) to/from Pozo de la Salud and walk along the very quiet road to the Arenas Blancas parking area (allow an extra 2.5km/35min *each way*)

This spectacular coastal path is really for everyone! Impressive lava formations, coastal arches, blow holes and weird rocks accompany you on the first leg of the walk; steep cliffs and a view of El Golfo fill the backdrop on the second part.

Start off at the signposted PARKING AREA FOR ARENAS BLANCAS (○) by following the clear track towards the coast. On the right is the small beach of **Arenas Blancas** with golden yellow sand. In the distance is the arc of El Golfo and nearby, on the black and bleak coastline the spa hotel of Pozo de la Salud. At a first fork, keep right; then, 50m/yds further on, keep left. The track now loops back to the left, and a clear stone-lined coastal path runs forward along the rocky cliffs. (This path will eventually form part of a GR coastal route round the island, but at time of writing is neither signposted nor waymarked.)

Follow this path to the left. After a few minutes you pass a

Halophytic vegetation at the start of the walk — saltwort (Schizogyne sericea), *sea fennel* (Astydamia latifolia) *and sea lavender* (Limonium pectinatum)

Arco de la Tosca

large BLOW HOLE on the right (❶; **10min**). Then the path moves inland for a while, to round a beautiful inlet. Another inlet follows (**20min**). Then you come to an elevated LAVA STREAM (❷; **25min**), where path rises and falls a little, crossing this tremendous lava flow. Ten minutes later you pass through a *kipuka* (**35min**) — a patch spared by the lava, where an abundance of the original vegetation shown on page 135 flourishes.

After another 10 minutes you pass some stone-lined fields on your left. A lovely *mirador* on a cliff, overlooking a large sea-arch, the **Arco de la Tosca**, is on your right (❸; **45min**). Here a track meets you from the left. Follow it down to the Playa del Verodal road (HI500), and turn left.

Walk back along this quiet road to the BLANCAS PARKING AREA (**1h10min**) — or continue on to **Pozo de la Salud** (●; **1h45min**) for your bus.

Walk 30: FRONTERA • MIRADOR DE JINAMA • ERMITA VIRGEN DE LA PEÑA • MIRADOR DE LA PEÑA

See also photos on pages 27, 132-133, 141, 142
Distance/time: 11km/6.8mi; 3h50min
Grade: ●● strenuous, with an ascent of 900m/3000ft and descent of 500m/1640ft. You must be sure-footed and have a head for heights. Take care crossing any loose gravel, whether on the path itself or the result of a landslide. Don't attempt after heavy rain (danger of rockfall). *Only worth the effort on fine days!* It can be very windy and cold on the *cumbre*. *Yellow/white waymarking (PR EH 8)*
Equipment: walking boots, sunhat (tied on!), sunglasses, suncream, long-sleeved shirt, long trousers, walking stick(s), fleece, windcheat, raingear, picnic, water

Transport: 🚕 by taxi or with friends to Frontera (27° 45.313'N, 18° 0.078'W) — or walk there from the Tigaday/Las Puntas junction Return by 🚐 (Línea 5) from the Mirador de la Peña (convenient departures at about 15.40, 18.40 Mon-Fri) or 🚕 telephone for a taxi

Short walk: Mirador de Jinama to Frontera (3.2km/2mi; 1h25min). ●● Easy, but steep descent of 900m/3000ft. Otherwise grade and equipment as main walk. Access 🚕 by taxi or with friends to the **Mirador de Jinama** (27° 45.770'N, 17° 58.853'W). Using the map to do the walk in reverse, descend the signposted path to **Frontera**. Return by 🚐 from Frontera, or call a taxi from Tigaday

This hike is one long view. From beginning to end you overlook the most stunning bay of the archipelago, El Golfo. And if that's not enough, the magnificent path underfoot is one of the most breathtaking in all the Canaries … both literally and visually.

Start the walk in the tiny village of **Frontera** (●): take the small road between the two bars opposite the CHURCH. At the fork 10m/yds uphill, keep left (signpost: 'JINAMA'). A steep narrow road takes you up a hillside stepped with vineyards. An amphitheatre of precipitous walls encircling the entire bay rises up before you. Your path will climb this very wall! A couple of minutes after passing a parking area with a couple of benches, the road bends sharp right (❶; **10min**). At the bend, turn left up a wide cobbled path (SIGNPOST). This fine centuries-old trail will take you up to the *mirador*. At a fork keep left and, on reaching the road again, go left for 20m/yds, then rejoin your path.

Thick stone walls flank the *camino*. Cross the road one last time, by a sign, 'CAMINO DE JINAMAR' (**20min**).

Above the vineyards the route dives into shady laurel woods and crosses the **Barranco las Esquinas**. The higher you climb, the more striking the views. The distant splash of white, high up the mountain wall near the end of the *cumbre*, is Sabinosa. The path, a work of art, ascends in a string of tortuous Zs. Here the precipitous cliffs are home to some rare endemics: *Bencomia sphaerocarpa*, *Crambe strigosa* and *Sideritis canariensis*, as well as the more common *Echium strictum* and *Aeonium holochrysum*.

A BALCONY VIEWPOINT (❷;

137

138 Landscapes of La Palma and El Hierro

'**Miradero**'; **1h20min**) makes a good rest stop, looking across the coastal plain of *malpais*. Pineapples are cultivated in the numerous greenhouses spread across it. The surrounding vegetation drips with moss and lichen. After ignoring a minor fork to the left, as you near the summit, a couple of stone tables and benches at a hillside *mirador* (❸; **1h50min**) provide a superb view over the gulf, framed by the *cumbre*. Fifteen minutes later, you reach the **Mirador de Jinama** (❹; **2h05min**; Picnic 30a), with a fountain (sometimes dry) in the hillside on the right, to the right of a chapel, the **Ermita de la Caridad**. *(The Short walk begins here.)* From the *mirador* you enjoy a superb view out over the whole bay, a dark lava coastline with jagged indentations contrasting with the bright greens and blues of the sea. The *cumbre* sweeps back out of the bay into a high wall fringed in laurels and heather.

From here the way is all downhill. Follow the road away from the *mirador*. When it swings

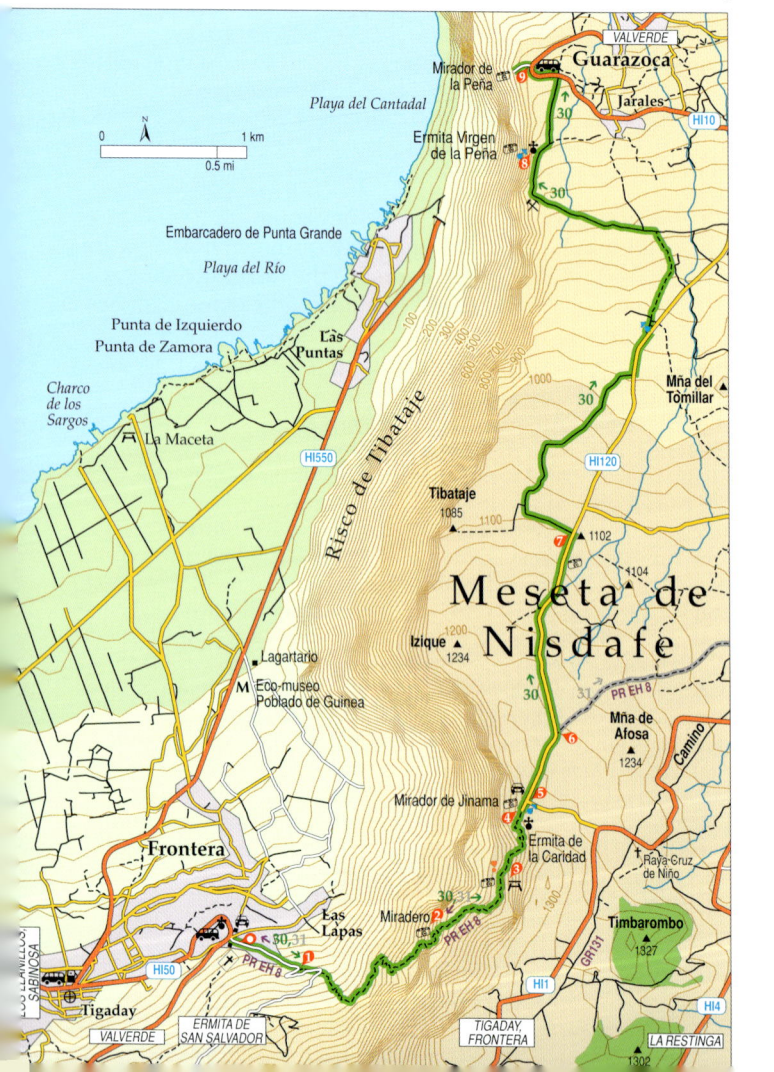

Ermita Virgen de la Peña

right towards the main road, continue STRAIGHT ON (**5**) along a country road. Ignore a track off left 50m/yds along and then the continuing PR EH 8 off right after another 50m (**6**; Walk 31). Now you're on the roof of the island, looking across the sloping **Meseta de Nisdafe** ruptured by a multitude of small volcanic cones. A maze of stone walls criss-cross the landscape.

Thirty minutes down the road, just after passing a fenced-off garden opposite a pint-sized VOLCANO (**7**; a good viewpoint; **2h35min**), turn left along a wide track. The track bumps its way between walled-off fields and grazing land, with the occasional plot of corn or potatoes.

Some five minutes along, the track bends right and acquires a tarmac surface, On meeting the ROAD again (**3h05min**), follow it to the left downhill for 200m/yds, then pick up your continuing path, which passes behind a MASSIVE WATER TANK. A minute along you meet a track coming from the right and follow it straight on, ignoring another track to the right after 50m/yds. When the track ends, go straight ahead, to pick up the old *camino* (between high stone walls). At the fork ahead, keep right on the main path. A few houses of Guarazoca can now be seen on the hillsides far below.

Less than 20 minutes from the road, you drop down onto a colourful, pink and mauve earthen track (signpost: 'LA PEÑA, PR EH 8'), and follow it to the left. A good 10 minutes later (having ignored all side-paths, tracks and roads), as you pass below an OLD QUARRY on the left (**3h35min**), the track bends right and becomes an asphalted lane at the edge of the crater.* Continue down the lane for another minute to the **Ermita Virgen de la Peña** (**8**; Picnic 18b), tucked into the side of the cliff just below. This chapel, shown above, is a superb quiet spot from which to enjoy the immense panorama.

From here continue down to the Mirador de la Peña, which you can already see — a cliff-hanging building housing a bar and restaurant, one of the most beautiful and impressive viewpoints in the Canarian archipelago. Follow the concrete lane down to the road, 15 minutes away, and turn left. Treat yourself to a well-earned drink at the **Mirador de la Peña** (**9**; **3h50min**), before telephoning for a taxi or catching the bus (Línea 5) at the entrance to the *mirador*.

---

*Some 80m/yds along you pass a path off left; it used to be part of the PR EH 8, and is still shown on many maps as a viable path. *Do not* attempt to descend this path, *it is broken away by landslides and exceedingly dangerous.*

Walk 31: FRONTERA • MIRADOR DE JINAMA • SAN ANDRES

See also photo on page 27
Distance/time: 8km/5mi; 2h50min
Grade: ●❗ strenuous, with an ascent of 900m/3000ft and descent of 600m/1970ft. You must be sure-footed and have a head for heights. Take care crossing any loose gravel, whether on the path itself or the result of a landslide. Don't attempt after heavy rain (danger of rockfall). *Only worth the effort on fine days!* It can be very windy and cold on the *cumbre*.

Yellow/white waymarking (PR EH 8)
Equipment: walking boots, sunhat (tied on!), sunglasses, suncream, long-sleeved shirt, long trousers, walking stick(s), fleece, windcheat, raingear, picnic, water
Transport: 🚖 by taxi or with friends to Frontera (27° 45.313'N, 18° 0.078'W) — or walk there from the Tigaday/Las Puntas junction. Return by 🚌 from San Andrés (Líneas 2 and 5) or telephone a Tigaday taxi from there.

The first half of this walk follows the same trail as Walk 30, the beautiful Camino de Jinama shown opposite and overleaf — an old transhumance trail, once used by shepherds twice a year. After the tough but beautiful ascent, during the second half of the walk you can stride out across the Nisdafe plateau to San Andrés, the island's highest village.

Start the walk in **Frontera** by following WALK 30 on page 141, the signposted PR EH 8 (❍). If you prefer to just use the map below (the trail is very well marked), take note of the following waypoints. The *camino* heads off left at the point where the road bends sharp right (❶; **10min**). A BALCONY VIEWPOINT (❷; '**Miradero**';

1h20min) makes a good rest stop, or you could take a break at the hillside *mirador* with stone tables and benches half an hour further up (❸; **1h50min**). You will know you are finally approaching the top of the climb when you pass a DYKE and look ahead to the view opposite: the path passes under an 'ARCHED' JUNIPER, with a MIRADOR

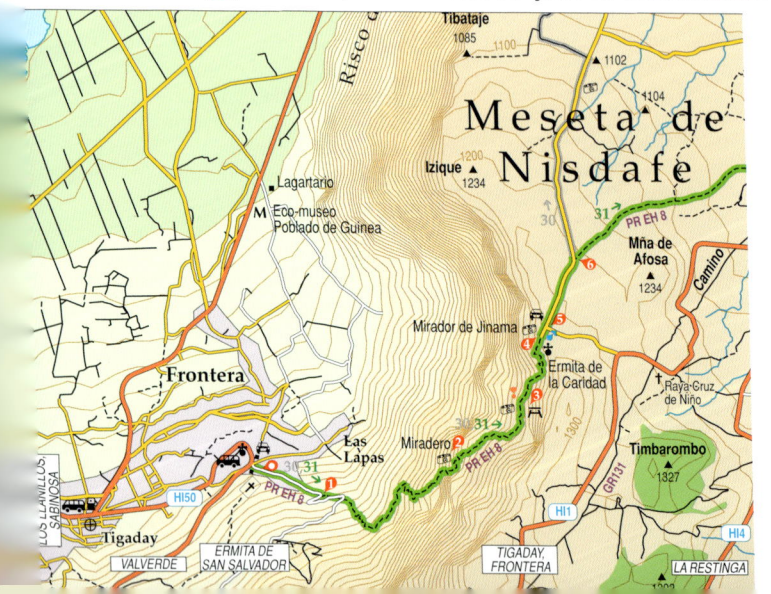

Almost there! We are just below the arched juniper, at the top of the trail.

to the left. There's a fountain and a chapel at the **Mirador de Jinama** (**4**; **2h05min**) — as well as a glorious view out over El Golfo … if the trade winds haven't yet carried in the clouds.

Follow the road away from the *mirador*. When it swings right towards the main road, continue STRAIGHT ON (**5**) along a country road. Seven minutes along, turn right on a wide, yellow/white waymarked path (**6**; signpost: 'PR EH 8, SAN ANDRÉS'). Some 30 minutes from the road, and shortly after the path has widened to a track, turn right at a fork. Two minutes later, when a track joins you from the right, follow it to the left (**7**; signpost: 'GR131, TIÑOR–VALVERDE, CAMINO DE LA VIRGEN'). This is the famous cross-island pilgrims' trail from the Ermita

Virgen de los Reyes to Valverde, but you won't stay on it for long. Just around the bend, turn right on another track. Several minutes later, you cross the Guarazoca road and enter **San Andrés**, passing the SCHOOL and the CHURCH. The BUS STOP (8; **2h50min**) is outside the shop on the left, where you meet the main HI1 (convenient departures on Mondays to Fridays, less so on weekends/holidays).

A work of art — the Camino de Jinama, an old *camino real*

Walk 32: CIRCUIT FROM THE FUENTE DE LA LLANÍA

Distance/time: 5km/3mi; 1h10min
Grade: ● easy, with an ascent of less than 100m/330ft; various colour-coded routes, but excellent signposting and easily followed
Equipment: walking shoes, fleece, jacket, long trousers, raingear, water
Transport: 🚗 by car only: park alongside the HI1 at the turn-off to the Ermita Virgen de los Reyes by the Fuente de la Llanía (27° 44.174'N, 17° 59.812'W)

This short hike is El Hierro's little gem. It starts with yet another stupendous view over the gulf — a view of which I never tire. Then it wanders in and out of 'fairy-tale' woods, where you feel you've stepped centuries back in time. Moss envelops the trees and thickly carpets the ground. And the crater of Hoya de Fileba comes as a pleasant surprise.

Start out on the HI1 at the JUNCTION FOR THE ERMITA DE LA VIRGEN DE LOS REYES (●). Walk north up the path at the left of the **Fuente de la Llanía** into the tall tree-heather (signpost: 'MIRADOR DE LA LLANÍA'). A short climb leads up to the **Mirador de la Llanía** (❶; **5min**; Picnic 20), a superb vantage point looking down over the line of villages strung out along the foot of the *cumbre*. The forested walls of the crater stretch out impressively on either side. Just before you reach the viewpoint, notice a LARGE STONE COLUMN WITH A SIGNPOST on it.

From this bald piece of gravelly hillside, go back to the signpost and turn left for 'BAILADERO DE LAS BRUJAS' (the Witches' Dancing Ground). The path edges its way through a small wood, the vegetation dripping with lichen and moss. Out on the *tupilli*-covered slopes again, ignore a path ascending to the left. Barely a minute further down this steep slope, the path swings left to dip down into a small hollow of pine trees. Here, at a SIGNPOSTED JUNCTION (❷), keep straight ahead via the **Bailadero de las Brujas** (❸), then taking a zig and a zag up a steep slope, to a VIEWPOINT (❹; **15min**) at the edge of a deepish crater — the **Hoya de Fileba**. This charcoal-grey crater is speckled with heather.

Return to the signpost at ❷ and now turn left for 'FUENTE DEL LOMO'. Look a short way along the road to the right, for a CULVERT. Walk through the culvert, then ascend the embankment on the left and continue along the path. Join a track and follow it to the right, to be greeted in a few minutes by a water tank — the **Fuente del Lomo** (❺). Unlike most other springs, you step *down* into this one.

With your back to the tank, take the path to the right, following a sign for 'PISTA EL BREZAL' (ORANGE ARROW). The slopes above the path are cushion-soft with moss, tempting you run your hands over the inclines. At a crossing, with signpost and arrows, go left. Mounting a slight rise, an old track with stones placed intermittently on either side comes underfoot. When you come to a cool grassy clearing with a signpost, cross a wide path and continue straight ahead on the right-hand side of the clearing along a track lined with stones. Follow this track, ignoring all side-paths and tracks, until it dips down into a gully. Just opposite a signpost with arrows, take a narrow path off to the right.

You cross a WOODEN BRIDGE (❻,

143

45min). The vegetation changes and patches of laurel forest take over from the heather. Not far beyond the bridge, you cross the HOYA DEL MORCILLO ROAD (**7**; HI40) and continue on the path signposted 'LA LLANIA'. At the fork that follows, wind your way up to the right. Ignore a path to the left as you follow a small gully running alongside on the right. Another junction follows: keep right and follow the path back to the junction by the **Fuente de la Llanía** (**1h10min**), where the walk began.

Back at your starting point, you may like to follow the road to the left for 0.7km, to enjoy a spectacular view of the volcanic landscape (add 20min).

View over El Golfo from the Mirador de la Llanía

Walk 33: FROM SAN ANDRES TO THE ARBOL GAROE

See also photo on pages 128-129

Distance/time: 7km/4.3mi; 1h50min

Grade: ● easy, with an ascent of less than 100m/330ft; easily followed (some *yellow/white PR and red/white GR signposting*). Note that these highlands can often disappear under cloud and mists, and it can be cold and windy; the walk is best kept for fine, cloudless days.

Equipment: walking shoes, fleece, jacket, long trousers, raingear, water

Transport: 🚌 Líneas 2 and 5 to/from San Andrés. By 🚗: park in San Andrés (27° 46.239'N, 17° 57.293'W)

Alternative walk: San Andrés — Arbol Santo — Tiñor (7.3km/4.4mi; 1h50min). ● Grade/equipment/access as above (by 🚌) Follow the main walk to the Arbol Garoé, then return to the fork first encountered at the 20min-point (**❷**; less than 30 minutes back; **1h20min**; signpost: 'GR131, TIÑOR, VALVERDE'). Turn sharp left here, across a sheltered basin. After a good five minutes, ignore a faint track to the left (●). Continue ahead for about another 200m/yds and, at a staggered junction, first turn left off the main track and then, at the fork that follows, keep right along a COBBLED TRAIL (●). Above lie fields of *tagasaste* (broom); its branches are cut for animal fodder. Soon you cross the MAIN HI1 ROAD (●) and descend to **Tiñor**, a quiet hamlet tucked away in a concealed valley. Entering the village, pass the CHURCH (●) and cross a road, to continue on the path, which descends to a driveway. Follow the drive back to the road, then keep straight on (right) for a couple of minutes, to regain the HI1 main road. There is a BUS STOP (●; **1h50min**) just here, or pick up your taxi.

A visit to the Arbol Garoé (or Arbol Santo — El Hierro's 'Holy Tree') is a must. There is a very interesting interpretation centre where you can learn about 'horizontal rain', but the tree itself is mystical — an ideal place to meditate.

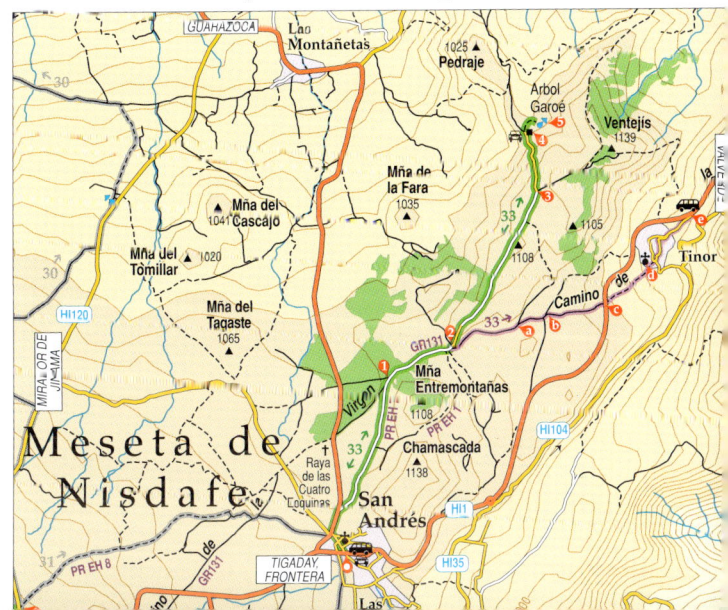

Leaving San Andrés from the BUS STOP (**0**), walk past the CHURCH on your right and the school to the HI10 road, where you at first follow the yellow/white-waymarked PR EH 7/11 to the right. After 150m/yds, turn right on a wide track (SIGNPOST), soon passing a row of volcanic cones on the right. After just under 1km along the track, you come to a junction where you meet the cross-island Camino de la Virgen (**1**): keep right (signpost: 'GR131, PR EH7, TIÑOR, VALVERDE, EL GAROE, EL MOCANAL, LA CALCOSA').

A little over five minutes later (**2**; **20min**), fork left uphill on asphalt (sign: 'ARBOL SANTO'). *(The Alternative walk leaves from this junction after visiting the tree.)* The way is tarred only for the first few minutes, then the beautiful earthen track shown below becomes your way. A basin of stone walls lies below to the right, and on the left volcanic mounds grow out of a tilting plateau. After 20 minutes, at the next fork, go left downhill (**3**; signpost: 'ARBOL SANTO/GAROE'). A tarred road leads you down to a PARKING AREA/VISITORS' CENTRE (**4**; open daily from 10.00-19.00, small entry fee). This is a fascinating place, where you can learn about the legends surrounding the tree but also about the phenomenon of 'horizontal rain'.

From the visitors' centre a well-trodden path heads right, round the hillside to **El Garoé**, the site of the original 'holy tree' (**5**; **Arbol Santo**; **55min**). Chronicles kept

Right: one of the old cisterns near the Arbol Garoé; below: this lovely orange track, lined with asphodels, leads through bucolic countryside to the Holy Tree.

during the time of the Spanish Conquest refer to this tree as being called Garoé and venerated by the native Bimbaches. It was an enormous *til* (an indigenous laurel), apparently with a trunk of a metre and a half in diameter. It stood at an altitude of about 1000m/3300ft, where there is the greatest concentration of rainfall and mists from the trade winds. Apparently its leaves were large enough to condense water to fill all the requirements of this quite small group of people. Remains of the many cisterns that the Bimbaches placed around the tree to collect the water can still be seen in the hillside (see right). It is also known that in 1610 a strong hurricane tore the tree down. A new *til*, shown on pages 132-133, was not replanted until 1949! It will take hundreds of years for it to achieve the girth of the original.

El Garoé is also the subject of many legends — one of which tells of the Bimbache maiden, Guarazoca, who fell in love with a Spanish soldier and revealed to him the source of their water. The tribe had been keeping the tree's location secret from the soldiers in the hope that they would leave the island because of its lack of water. For this betrayal she was punished with death.

From here retrace your steps to **San Andrés (1h50min)**.

Walk 34: FUENTE DE LA LLANIA • MIRADOR DE LAS PLAYAS • LA TORRE • SAN ANDRES

Distance/time: 12.1km/7.5mi; 3h
Grade: ● easy, with ascents of about 250m/820ft and descents of 400m/1300ft overall. Note that these highlands often disappear under cloud and mists, and it can be cold and windy; the walk is best kept for fine, cloudless days.
Equipment: walking boots, sunhat, suncream, raingear, long-sleeved shirt, long trousers, windcheat, fleece, picnic, plenty of water
Transport: 🚗 by car: park beside the HI1 at the turn-off to the Ermita Virgen de los Reyes by the Fuente de la Llanía (27° 44.174'N, 17° 59.812'W). Return on 🚐 Línea 2 or 5 from San Andrés.

The pine trees in El Pinar are among the most majestic in the archipelago. Just as bonsai is striking in its contrived, pint-sized beauty, so the *Pinus canariensis* is striking in its natural grandeur. From the heights of El Pinar you descend to another of El Hierro's picture-postcard *miradores*, before gradually climbing to a countryside where time stands still. If you've the time, I highly recommend tacking on Walk 33 — or, if you're the adventurous type, leave this walk at Tajace and pick up Walk 35.

Start the walk at the turn-off to the Ermita de la Virgen de los Reyes a few metres west of the **Fuente de la Llanía** (O). Just at the start of this road (the HI45), take the path to the left signposted 'SENDERO DE LA LLANIA'. Follow the GREEN ARROWS of this circular walk to where it crosses the HOYA DEL MORCILLO ROAD. (But if you would like to spend an extra 20 minutes in this fairy-tale forest, then before continuing ahead, turn right with the RED AND BLUE ARROWS, to make an extra loop between ● and ●, back to the Hoya del Morcillo road.)

Join the HI45 ROAD (①) and turn right for 15 minutes. By several LARGE PINES (**30min**), note a track turning left into the forest. Pass it by but, 90m/yds below it, at a bend in the road, TURN LEFT (②) on a minor track. After 50m/yds, at a fork, go left. You dip into a hollow to the left, then mount a second, parallel crest. When a track joins from the left, keep downhill. This track will take you straight down to the El Pinar road. (Even if you lose trace of the track, just keep straight downhill and you will come to the road.) In this cool, shady forest, you're surrounded by grand pines. The forest floor is 'whistle-clean', a

Crossing the plateau through walled-in pastures, on the approach to San Andrés

characteristic of a true Canary wood.

A little over five minutes down the track, you cross a *canal*. Less than 10 minutes later you cross the EL PINAR ROAD (HI4): keep straight on towards the STONE WALL ahead, crossing a WATER PIPE en route. Then turn left alongside the wall and, *without a path*, remain between the pipe and the wall (closer to the pipe in the last few metres) until, after 15 minutes, you meet the ROAD TO THE MIRADOR DE LAS PLAYAS. Turn right

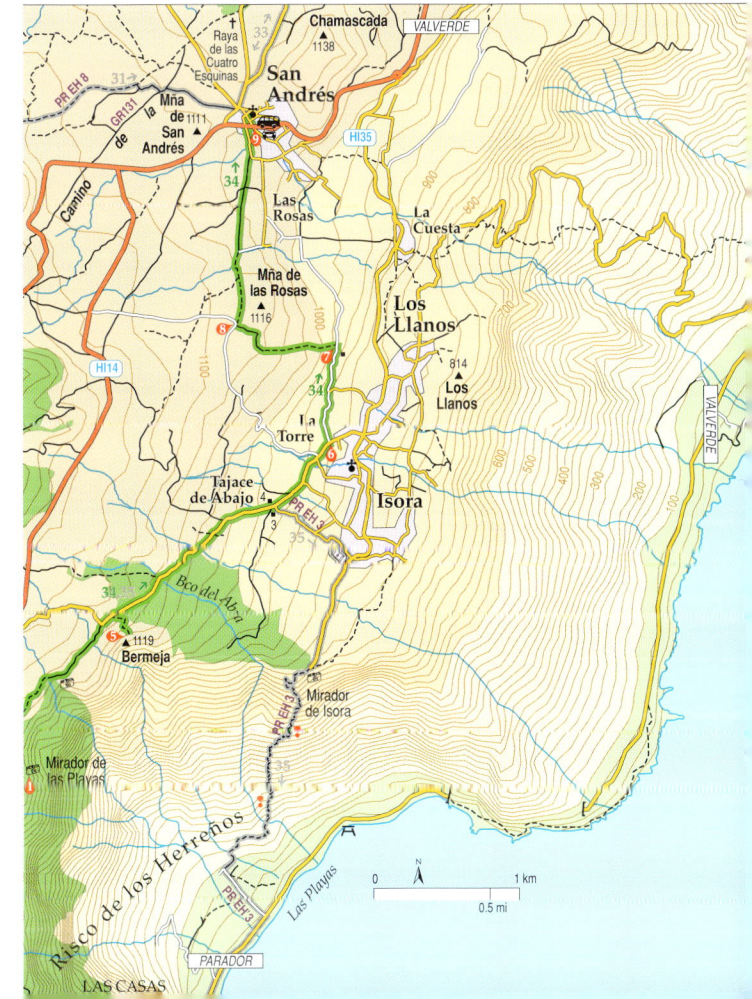

SOME PLANTS YOU MAY SEE ON THESE ISLANDS

Senecio sp.

Aeonium manriqueorum

Taginaste (Echium decaisnei)

Greenovia aurea

Codeso (Adenocarpus foliolosus)

Prickly poppy

Cerrajón (Sonchus ortunoi)

Cardón (Euphorbia canariensis)

Margarita (Argyranthemum)

Rock rose (Cistus)

Palo sangre (Sonchus tectifolius)

Prickly pear (Optunia ficus-indica)

Valo (Plocama pendula)

Canary bellflower

Retama (Spartocytisus supranubius)

Sea fennel (Crithmum latifolium)

Lavandula pinnata

Peorera (Andryala cheiranthifolia)

Century plant (Agave americana)

150

Walk 34: From the Fuente de la Llanía to San Andrés 151

here, passing the turn-off right for the PR EH 3 (**3**) to Las Casas after 100m/yds. A few minutes later you reach the **Mirador de las Playas** (**4**; **1h10min**; Picnic 34). The narrow curving bay set at the foot of 1000m/3300ft-high eroded cliffs is Las Playas. The *parador* is an obvious landmark in this desolate, isolated corner of the island.

From the *mirador* return along the road for 200m/yds, then turn right on a path signposted 'PR EH 3 LAS PLAYAS, LA CUESTA'; this initially dips down, before heading uphill between stone walls. The small evergreen shrub predominant in the fields here is white broom *(escobon)*. Less than 20 minutes from the *mirador* you join a track very near the edge of the cliff. This becomes asphalted and soon ascends to the HI40 ROAD (**1h40min**; signpost: 'PR EH3 LAS PLAYAS, LA CUESTA'). Turn right on the road and, a minute along, turn right again to climb nearby **Montaña Bermeja** (**5**), an orange volcanic mound. From its summit there are fine views over the farming village of Isora on the slopes ahead.

You will now continue along this quiet country road for around 30 minutes, to La Torre. *(Walk 35 turns off the road about 20 minutes downhill, opposite house No 4 in Tajace de Abajo.)* In **La Torre** (**2h10min**) you cross a concrete ford in the road. Barely two minutes later, turn left along a road called **Calle La Ladera** (**6**). When you join a road ascending from the right, continue uphill. Some 15 minutes from La Torre (**2h25min**), 150m/yds past a beautiful, isolated *casa rural*, take the first left, a track ascending a narrow *barranco* (**7**). A minute up, an old cobbled *camino* becomes your way. The path climbs alongside the gully, before entering it briefly. Two minutes up the gully, leave it (beside a volcanic cone), and continue left as the path crosses a plateau. At a T-junction with a track (**2h45min**), turn right. Just before stepping onto an asphalt road, TURN 90° RIGHT on a wide path (**8**). Walled-in pastures stretch across this tableland. San Andrés comes into sight across the stone walls, spread around the base of a volcanic cone.

Soon you reach a wide dry stream bed: turn right here, quickly coming to a road which you follow straight ahead (left). Follow it to a T-junction on the edge of **San Andrés**. Go left here and, after a few minutes, you come to the MAIN HI1 ROAD. I enjoy the noisy back-slapping BAR LA IGUALDAD along to the right. But for the bus, turn right on the main road, then take the next left. Turn left to the BUS STOP (**9**; **3h05min**) in front of the CHURCH.

Verode (Kleinia neriifolia)

Ranunculus cortusfolius

Red-flowering tabaiba (Euphorbia atropurpurea)

Vinagrera (Rumex lunaria)

35: FUENTE DE LA LLANIA • MIRADOR DE ISORA • PARADOR

Distance/time: 13km/8mi; 4h25min
Grade: ●❗ strenuous, with a steep, rough, vertiginous descent of 800m/2600ft from the *mirador*. You must be sure-footed and have a head for heights. Do not attempt in wet or very windy weather. The walk is sometimes *closed* due to rockfall or landslides. *Yellow/white waymarking (PR EH 3)*
Equipment: walking boots, sunhat, suncream, raingear, long-sleeved shirt, long trousers, windcheat, fleece, swimming things, picnic, plenty of water
Transport: 🚗 by car: park beside the HI1 at the turn-off to the Ermita Virgen de los Reyes by the Fuente de la Llanía (27° 44.174'N, 17° 59.812'W). Return on 🚌 Línea 7 from the *parador* (departs at about 17.30 daily) or telephone for a taxi.

Looking up at the Herreños cliffs from the *parador*, you'd never imagine a footpath tackling these heights. But there *is* a good trail ... for very sure-footed, adventurous hikers; the less confident of spirit and limb could go to the Mirador de Isora for the astounding view and from there use the map on pages 152-153 to follow Walk 34 to San Andrés.

Start out by following WALK 34 to **Tajace de Abajo** (**6**; **1h55min**). As you come upon the houses, turn right immediately after building No 3 (opposite house No 4). There is a signpost here, 'PR EH 3, LAS PLAYAS, LA CUESTA, VEREDA DEL RISCO'. Follow the asphalted road straight downhill until you come to a T-junction by the fenced-in football stadium on your right. Turn right here; after 10 minutes you come to the **Mirador de Isora** (**7**; **2h25min**).

Your ongoing path (flanked by stone walls) begins on the far side of the viewpoint (SIGNPOST), and ascends to the crest opposite —

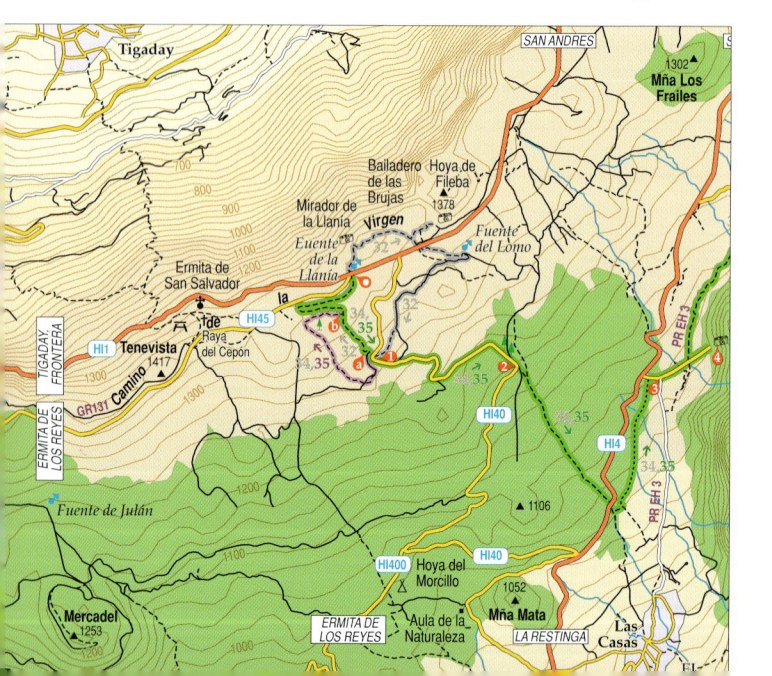

Walk 35: From the Fuente de la Llanía to the Parador   153

then you begin the descent. A couple of minutes from the *mirador*, ignore a faint turning to the right. Take utmost care as you descend this very steep and slippery path, and leave any gates as you find them.

On entering the bed of the **Barranco del Abra** (8; **4h**), the PR EH 3 path goes off to the right. Either keep left downhill here on a faint path waymarked with white dots and small cairns, floundering in and out of the stream bed, or continue on the PR EH 3 as shown on the map. When you meet the road by either route, the *parador* is a short way to the right (9; **4h25min**).

Plunging view from the Mirador de Isora down onto the isolated Playas, a curving line of stony beaches hidden in the sheer coastline. The parador *and a few solitary houses are the sole occupants of this barren, inhospitable stretch of arcing coastline. See also photo overleaf.*

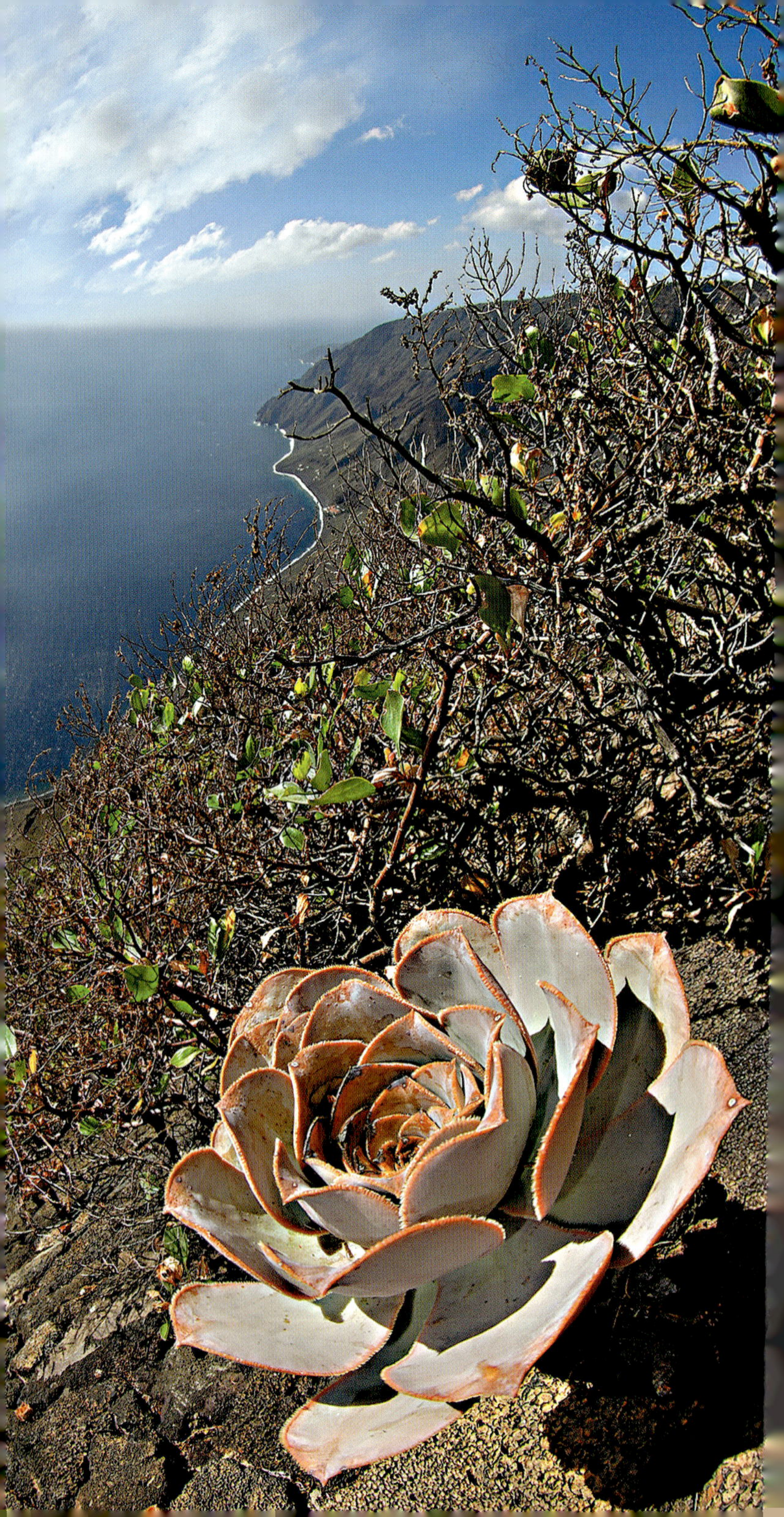

BUS TIMETABLES, FLIGHTS AND FERRIES

LA PALMA — BUSES

For a list of all the island's bus lines (38 at press date), with timetables and a route maps, see **www.tilp.es**. See page 7 for more information. Buses lines are listed numerically below.

Line 23: Fuencaliente (Los Canarios) to El Faro; daily; journey time 30min
Departs Fuencaliente: 09.15, 11.15, 13.15, 15.15, 17.15
Departs El Faro: 09.45, 11.45, 13.45, 15.45, 17.45

Line 27: Los Llanos to Puerto de Tazacorte; daily; journey time 15min
Departs Los Llanos: 08.45 and hourly at 45min past the hour until 21.45, **but no departure at 16.45**
Departs Puerto de Tazacorte: 08.00 and hourly on the hour until 22.00, **but no departure at 14.00**

Line 100: Santa Cruz to Barlovento; daily; journey time 55min-1h

Mondays to Fridays

Santa Cruz	Tenagua	Puntallana	La Galga	Los Sauces	Barlovento
06.15	06.30	06.35	06.45	06.50	07.15

and hourly at 15min past the hour until 21.15

Barlovento	Los Sauces	La Galga	Puntallana	Tenagua	Santa Cruz
06.25	06.35	06.55	07.05	07.10	07.25

and hourly at 25min past the hour until 21.25

Saturdays, Sundays and holidays

Santa Cruz	Tenagua	Puntallana	La Galga	Los Sauces	Barlovento
06.15	06.30	06.35	06.45	06.50	07.15

and every two hours at 15min past the hour until 20.15

Barlovento	Los Sauces	La Galga	Puntallana	Tenagua	Santa Cruz
07.25	07.35	07.55	08.05	08.10	08.25

and every two hours at 25min past the hour until 21.25

Line 110: Los Llanos to Puntagorda; daily; journey time 55min-1h

Mondays to Fridays

Los Llanos	Tazacorte	Pto Tazacorte	Tijarafe	Tinizara	Puntagorda
06.15	06.25	06.30	06.50	07.00	07.10

*and hourly at 15min past the hour until 21.15, **but no bus at 15.15***

Puntagorda	Tinizara	Tijarafe	Pto Tazacorte	Tazacorte	Los Llanos
06.25	06.35	06.45	07.05	07.10	07.20

*and hourly at 25min past the hour until 21.25, **but no bus at 20.25***

Saturdays, Sundays and holidays

Los Llanos	Tazacorte	Pto Tazacorte	Tijarafe	Tinizara	Puntagorda
06.15	06.25	06.30	06.50	07.00	07.10

*and hourly at 15min past the hour until 21.15, **but no bus at 15.15***

Puntagorda	Tinizara	Tijarafe	Pto Tazacorte	Tazacorte	Los Llanos
06.25	06.35	06.45	07.05	07.10	07.20

*and hourly at 25min past the hour until 21.25, **but no bus at 20.25***

Line 120: Barlovento to Puntagorda; daily; journey time 1h25min

Mondays to Fridays

Barlovento	Gallegos	Franceses	Garafia	Las Tricias	Puntagorda
05.30	05.40	05.55	06.40	06.50	06.55

and every two hours on the half hour until 19.30

Puntagorda	Las Tricias	Garafia	Franceses	Gallegos	Barlovento
07.30	07.35	07.45	08.30	08.45	08.55

and every two hours on the half hour until 19.30

Left: Mirador de Isora

156　Landscapes of La Palma and El Hierro

Line 120: Barlovento to Puntagorda, *continued*

Saturdays, Sundays and holidays

Barlovento	Gallegos	Franceses	Garafía	Las Tricias	Puntagorda
11.30	11.40	11.55	12.40	12.50	12.55
15.30	15.40	15.55	16.40	16.50	16.55
19.30	19.40	19.55	20.40	20.50	20.55
Puntagorda	Las Tricias	Garafía	Franceses	Gallegos	Barlovento
09.30	09.35	09.45	10.30	10.45	10.55
13.30	13.35	13.45	14.30	14.45	14.55
17.30	17.35	17.45	18.30	18.45	18.55

Line 200: Santa Cruz to Fuencaliente via Mazo*; daily; journey time 50min

Departs Santa Cruz: 06.15**, 08.15, 10.15, 12.15, 14.15, 16.15, 18.15, 20.15, 22.30
Departs Fuencaliente: 06.40**, 09.00, 11.00, 13.00, 15.00, 17.00, 19.00, 21.00
*Calls at Mazo 15-20min after departing Santa Cruz, 35-40min after departing Fuencaliente
**Mon-Fri only

Line 201: Santa Cruz to Fuencaliente via Mazo*; daily; journey time 50min

Departs Santa Cruz: 07.15**, 09.15, 11.15**, 13.00, 14.15**, 15.15**, 17.15, 19.15**, 21.15
Departs Fuencaliente: 06.00**, 06.40**, 08.00, 10.00, 12.00**, 13.45, 16.00**, 18.00, 20.00**
*Calls at Mazo 10-15min after departing Santa Cruz, 30-35min after departing Fuencaliente
**Mon-Fri only

Line 210: Los Llanos to Fuencaliente; daily; journey time 30min

Departs Los Llanos: 06.00*, 08.15, 10.15, 12.15, 14.15, 16.15, 18.15, 20.15
Departs Fuencaliente: 07.15*, 09.15, 11.15, 13.15, 14.15, 15.15, 17.15, 19.15, 21.15
**Mon-Fri only

Line 300: Santa Cruz to Los Llanos* via the *cumbre*; daily; journey time 45min

Mondays to Fridays
Departs Santa Cruz: 06.10, 06.40 and then every 10 and 40min past the hour until 22.40
Departs Los Llanos: 06.05, 06.35 and then every 5 and 35min past the hour until 22.35

Saturdays, Sundays and holidays
Departs Santa Cruz: 06.10 and then every 10min past the hour until 20.10, then 21.40, 22.40
Departs Los Llanos: 05.35 and then every 35min past the hour until 22.35

*Stops at 'Túnel de la cumbre' 15-20min after leaving Santa Cruz, 30-35min after leaving Los Llanos; stops at the Visitors' Centre 20-25min after leaving Santa Cruz, 20-25min after leaving Los Llanos

At about 35 minutes along Walk 26, approaching El Palmar, you look across the northwest corner of the island (left) and may spot a lonely billy goat (right).

EL HIERRO — BUSES

Buses are run by the Sociedad Cooperativa de Transportes de Viajeros del Hierro (4, Calle El Molino, Valverde; www.transhierro.es). The website has an English version. As of press date, the website was a bit tedious to use, however, as there were no weekly timetables to view: one had to choose the specific date of travel to see bus times. However, there are good route maps showing all stops.

Línea 1: Around Valverde; Mon-Sat only; circuit takes 20min
Mon-Sat only departs Valverde 08.00, 09.00, 09.40, 12.00, 12.40, 15.00*, 16.50*, 18.00*
* not on Saturdays

Línea 2: Valverde to El Pinar via San Andrés and Tiñor; daily; journey time 30min

Mondays to Fridays

El Pinar	San Andrés	Valverde
07.10	07.20	07.40
09.30	09.40	10.00
12.00	12.10	12.30
14.40	14.50	15.10
17.00	17.10	17.30
19.30	19.40	20.00

Valverde	San Andrés	El Pinar
08.00	08.20	08.30
10.30	10.50	11.00
13.10	13.30	13.40
15.30	15.50	16.00
18.00	18.20	18.30
21.30	21.50	22.00

Saturdays, Sundays and holidays

El Pinar	San Andrés	Valverde
07.10	07.20	07.40
09.30	09.40	10.00
12.00	12.10	12.30
14.40	14.50	15.10
19.30	19.40	20.00

Valverde	San Andrés	El Pinar
08.00	08.20	08.30
10.30	10.50	11.00
13.10	13.30	13.40
18.30	18.50	19.00
21.30	21.50	22.00

Línea 3: El Golfo to Valverde (from Frontera bus station, via Las Puntas); journey time about 25min
Mon-Fri: Departs Frontera 07.15, 09.30, 12.00, 14.45, 16.15, 21.00; departs Valverde 07.45, 10.00, 12.30, 15.15, 16.45, 21.30
Sat, Sun and holidays: Departs Frontera 07.15, 09.30, 12.00, 15.15, 18.00, 21.00; departs Valverde 07.45, 10.00, 12.30, 15.45, 18.30, 21.30

Línea 4: Around Frontera; daily; circuit takes 30min
Departs Frontera 07.30, 09.30, 12.00, 13.00, 16.30, 17.30

Línea 5: Valverde — San Andrés — Mirador de Isora; daily; journey time 40min
Mon-Fri: Departs Valverde 08.00, 10.00, 13.10, 15.00, 18.00, 21.30; departs Mirador de Isora 07.00, 09.00, 11.00, 14.00, 16.00, 20.30
Sat, Sun and holidays: Departs Valverde 08.00, 10.00, 13.10, 18.30, 21.30; departs Mirador de Isora 07.00, 09.00, 11.00, 16.00, 20.30

158 Landscapes of La Palma and El Hierro

Línea 7: Valverde — *Parador;* daily; journey time 30min
Mon-Fri: Departs Valverde 07.00, 09.30, 11.30, 13.00, 15.30, 17.00; departs Parador 07.30, 10.00, 12.00, 13.30, 16.00, 17.30
Sat, Sun and holidays: Departs Valverde 07.00, 09.30, 11.30, 13.00, 17.00; departs Parador 07.30, 10.00, 12.00, 13.30, 17.30

Línea 12: Frontera — Sabinosa — Pozo de la Salud; daily; journey time 30min
Mon-Fri: Departs Frontera 08.30, 11.00, 13.40, 15.15, 18.30, 22.00; departs Pozo de la Salud 06.30, 09.00, 11.30, 14.10, 15.45, 19.00
Sat, Sun and holidays: Departs Frontera 08.30, 11.00, 13.40, 19.00, 22.00; departs Pozo de la Salud 06.30, 09.00, 11.30, 14.10, 19.30

FLIGHTS TO LA PALMA AND EL HIERRO

At time of writing there are **direct flights** with TUI from London Gatwick and Manchester to **Santa Cruz de la Palma** on Thursdays throughout the year. Flights via Madrid and Barcelona with Iberia and other carriers are another option. There are ***no direct flights to El Hierro***, so those visiting *only* El Hierro usually fly via Tenerife or Gran Canaria.

If you cannot fly direct, it makes most sense to fly to either island via Gran Canaria, because the same airport is used for incoming international flights and outgoing local flights. In contrast, almost all flights from the UK to Tenerife are into Reina Sofía airport in the *south*, whereas the Binter flights to La Palma and El Hierro are out of Los Rodeos airport in the *north* (an expensive taxi transfer). See www.titsa.com for buses between the airports (lines 340/343) or local buses into Santa Cruz (line 111) and from there to Los Rodeos (lines 102, 107, 108).

INTER-ISLAND TRAVEL

You can travel between the islands by air or ferry but, unfortunately, arrangements seem to change every year — some years the only direct connection is by air, other years by ferry.

By plane: At time of writing it is *not* possible to fly direct between the islands — one has to travel via Tenerife. Flights are frequent and connections good, making a total journey time of just over two hours. Still, that compares very badly with the direct flights which used to run twice a week and take only 15-20 minutes!

Keep your eye on the website **www.bintercanarias.com**, to see if the direct flights have been resumed. All information about current flights via Tenerife is on the same website, and flights can be booked online — or contact your travel agent *before you go* (flights may be full if you wait until you are on the islands to book).

By ferry: At the time of writing the only ferry connection between La Palma and El Hierro is via Tenerife (Los Cristianos). Two ferry companies currently serve these routes: Naviera Armas (**www.navieraarmas.com**) and Fred Olsen Lines (**www.fredolsen.es**). Ferry bookings can be made online, at travel agencies before you go or once you are on the islands — or at the ferry kiosks at the Santa Cruz and Valverde ports.

Index

This index contains geographical entries only; for other entries, see Contents, page 3. **Bold type** indicates a photograph; *italic type* indicates a map. Both may be in addition to a text reference on the same page. 'TT' refers to *transport timetables.*

LA PALMA

Barlovento 9, 10, 13, 16, *42,* 45, 46, *47,* 121, 125, 127, TT 155, 156
   Laguna de Barlovento 10, 13, 16, **46,** 47, *48*
Barranco de La Galga 14, **63,** *64,* **64-5,** *66*
Barranco de las Angustias 10, **24-5,** 103, **105,** *106-7,* 109, **110,** *111,* 112, 113
Barranco de Ribanseras del Castro *106-7,* **108,** 109, *111*
Barranco del Agua 14, 15, 45, 49, 51, *52,* 53, 54, *56-7,* 59, *71,* **73**
Barranco Río Almedro Amargo *106-7,* **108,** *111*
Breña Alta *see* San Pedro
Caldera de Taburiente 5, 10, 12, 18, 22, 24, 25, 54, 74, 86, **100,** 101, 102, 104, *106-7,* 109, *111,* 112, 125
Casa del Monte 54, *56-7,* 59, *60-1*
Cascada de Colores *106-7,* 109, 110, *111,* **111**
Cráter del Duraznero 97, 98
Cruce del Refugio *78, 88-9,* 109, 110
Cumbre Nueva 23, *75, 77, 78, 79, 82,* 83, 86, **87,** *88-9*
Cumbre Vieja 76, *77,* 95
Dos Aguas 104, **105,** *106-7,* 109, 110
El Fayal 10, 24, **25,** 121, *125*
El Palmar 125, 126, *127*
El Paso 19, 22, 76, 77, 80, 86, 96, 102, *106-7*
   National Park Visitors' Centre 19, 74, *75, 77, 78, 79, 82, 85*
El Rodeo 102, *103*
Ermita de la Virgen del Pino **22,** 74, 76, *77, 78, 79, 82*
Fuencaliente 2, 19, 20, 21, 34, 90, 91, *92,* 97, 99, TT 155, 156
Faro de Fuencaliente **2,** 20, 21, 90, 91, *92,* **92,** 93, 94, TT 155
Franceses 16, 17, 18, TT 155, 156
Gallegos 16, *42,* 43, 47, 127, TT 155, 156
Garafía 13, 18, 125, **126,** *127,* TT 155, **156**

Hoyo de Mazo 19
Juan Adalid 125, *127*
La Cumbrecita 19, 22, **36,** *75, 77,* 80, **81, 82,** 102, *103, 106-7*
La Galga 13, *56-7, 60-1,* 63, *64,* 65, *66,* TT 155
   Cubo de La Galga *64,* 65, *66*
La Palmita *42,* 43
La Pared Vieja 9, 19, 23, 83, 84, *85,* 87, *88-9,* 95
La Tosca 9, 16, *42,* 43, 44, 136
Las Indias 19, 20, 21, 90, 91, *92,* 93, *97*
Las Lomadas 14, *47, 48,* 49, 51, 52, 54, *56-7,* 59, *60-1,* 62
Las Tricias 18, 121, **122-3,** *123, 124,* TT 155, 156
Llano del Jable 10, 23, *78, 79,* **84-5,** 86, 95, 96
Lomo de los Mestres *75, 79, 82,* 83, 84, *85,* 87, *88-9*
Los Brecitos 24, 25, 103, 104, *106-7,* 109, *111*
Los Canarios *see* Fuencaliente
Los Llanos 22, 23, 24, 25, 34, 96, 102, *106-7,* 112, 114, 117, 121, TT 155, 156
Los Sauces 13, 15, 45, *47,* 48, 51, *56-7, 60-1,* 62, 68, TT 155
Los Tilos 9, 13, 14, **40-1,** *48,* 49, **50,** *51, 52,* 53, 54, 55, *56-7,* 58, 59, 62, 64, 104
Mazo 19, 20, 38, 87, *88-9,* TT 156
Mirador de las Barandas 45, *47,* **50, 51,** 52, **53,** *56-7, 60-1,*
Mirador de las Indias 21, *92, 97*
Mirador El Time 24, 25, 112, *113*
Mirador Espigón Atravesado *52,* 58, *56-7, 60-1*
Mirador La Cumbrecita *75, 82*
Mirador La Tosca 9, 16, *42,* 43, **44**
Morro de la Era 19, 109, **110,** *111*
Nacientes de Cordero y Marcos 54, **55,** *56-7,* **38-9,** *60-1,* 62
Observatorio Astrofísico 13, **16-7,** 18
Parque Cultural La Zarza 13

159

Pico Bejenado 22, 102, *103*, **103**, *106-7*
Pico Birigoyo *95*, **100**, *101*
Pico de la Nieve 18, 71, 74, *75*, 76, 77, 82, 102
Piscinas de la Fajana 16, 17
Playa de los Cancajos 19, 34
Playa de Taburiente 76, 103, *106-7*, 110
Playa de Zamora 21
Poris de Candelaria ('Pirates' Cove') 114, **115**, **116**, *116*
Puerto de Tazacorte 25, **112-3**, *113*, TT 155
Puntagorda 10, 18, 24, 25, 117, 121, *123*, TT 155, 156
Puntallana **8-9**, 13, 23, *67*, 67, 68, **69**, *70*, 70, *71*, 72, 73, TT 155
Refugio El Pilar 9, 19, 23, 78, *79*, 83, *85*, 86, *95*, **96**, 101
Refugio Punta de los Roques 74, *75*, *76*, 77
Reventón Pass 77, 78, **79**, *79*, 82
Río Taburiente *106-7*, 108, 109, 110, *111*
Roque de los Muchachos 13, 16, 18, 76
Roque de Teneguía 21, 90, **91**, *92*, 93, 94
Ruta de los Volcanes **5**, *33*, 83, *95*, **96**, *97*, **98-9**, **100**, 101
San Antonio 13, 17, 19, 20, 90, 93, 114
San Isidro 9, 23, 84, 87, 88
San Pedro (Breña Alta) 23, 84
Santa Cruz 7, 10, 13, **14-5**, 19, 23, 34, 156, 158
town plan with touring map
Santuario de Las Nieves 19, 23
Somada del Palo 65, 66, *106-7*, 108, 154
Tajuya 22
Tazacorte 24, 25, TT 155
Tenagua 71, 72
Tigalate 20
Tijarafe 25, 114, *116*, *117*, 119, TT 155
Tinizara 25, *117*, **118-9**, *120*, TT 155
Volcán de San Antonio 90, 93
Volcán de Teneguía **20**, 21, **90-1**, *92*, 93, 94
Volcán Deseada *95*, *97*, 98
Volcán Martín **5**, *97*, **98-9**

EL HIERRO
Arbol Santo (El Garoë) 31, **128-9**, *145*, **146-7**, **147**
Arenas Blancas 27, **135**, *136*, **136**
Bailadero de las Brujas 143, *144*
Cala de Tacorón 11, 26, 29, **30**
Cruz de los Reyes 26, 29
El Golfo 10, **27**, 28, 30, *130-1*, 132, 133, 134, 135, *136*, 137, 141, 144, TT 157
El Pinar 11, 26, 29, 30, 148, 149, TT 157

El Sabinar **1**, 28, 132, *134*
Ermita de la Caridad 138
Ermita de la Virgen de los Reyes 11, 17, 26, 29, **132-3**, *134*, 142, 143, 148, 152
Ermita Virgen de la Peña 10, 26, 137, *138*, **139**
Faro de Orchilla 26, 28
Frontera 10, 11, 26, **27**, 29, 34, 137, *138*, *140-1*, TT 157, 158
Fuente de la Llanía 10, 11, 143, *144*, **148-9**, 151, *152-3*
Fuente del Lomo 143, *144*
Guarazoca 10, 30, *138*, 139, 142, 147
Guinea, Eco-museum **29**
Hoya de Fileba 143, *144*
Hoya del Morcillo 11, 26, 29, 30, *144*, 148
Isora 31, *148-9*, 151, *152-3*, TT 157
La Dehesa 26, 28, 131, 132, 133, *134*
La Restinga 11, 29, 30, 34
La Torre 148, 151
Las Casas (El Pinar) 29, 149
Las Playas *148-9*, *152-3*, **153**
Las Puntas 26, 134, 137, 140, TT 157
Meseta de Nisdafe *138*, *140-1*, 145
Mirador de Bascos 132, 133, *134*
Mirador de Isora 31, *152-3*, **153**, TT 157
Mirador de Jinama 10, 26, 30, 137, *138*, *140-1*, **141**, **142**
Mirador de la Llanía 29, 143, *144*, **144**, *148-9*
Mirador de la Peña 10, 26, 137, *138*, 139
Mirador de las Playas 11, 30, *148-9*, **150**, *152-3*
Mocanal 26, 31, 146
Montaña Bermeja 151
Pista al Derrabado *130-1*
Playa del Verodal 11, 26, **27**, 136
Pozo de la Salud 28, 114, *130-1*, 134, 135, *136*, TT 158
Pozo de las Calcosas 26, 31
Puerto de la Estaca 11, 31
Sabinosa 26, **27**, *130-1*, **131**, 132, 133, *134*, 137, TT 158
San Andrés 11, 15, 26, 30, 31, 68, *140-1*, 142, *145*, 146, 147, *148-9*, 151, 152, TT 157
Taibique (El Pinar) 26, 29
Tamaduste 31
Tigaday 26, **27**, 29, 31, 34, 130, 137, *138*, 140
Timijiraque 11
Tiñor 31, **145**, 146, TT 157
Valverde 7, 26, 28, 29, 31, 141, 142, 145, 146, TT 157, 158
town plan with touring map